SUCCEEDING in MUSIC

A BUSINESS HANDBOOK
FOR PERFORMERS,
SONGWRITERS,
AGENTS, MANAGERS
& PROMOTERS

Backbeat
Books
San Francisco

Published by Backbeat Books
600 Harrison Street, San Francisco, CA 94107
www.backbeatbooks.com
E-mail: books@musicplayer.com
An imprint of Music Player Network
United Entertainment Media, Inc.

Distributed to the book trade in the US and Canada by
Publishers Group West, 1700 Fourth Street, Berkeley, CA 94710

Distributed to the music trade in the US and Canada by
Hal Leonard Publishing, P.O. Box 13819, Milwaukee, WI 53213

Cover Design: The Visual Group
Text Design and Composition: Michael Cutter
Production Editor: Michael Baughan
Copy Editor: Julie Herrod-Lumsden

Library of Congress Cataloging in Publication Data:
Stiernberg, John.

    Succeeding in music: a business handbook for performers, songwriters, agents,
managers, and promoters / by John Stiernberg.

       p. cm.

    Includes bibliographical references

    ISBN 0-87930-702-1 (alk. paper)

    1. Music trade—United States. 2. Music trade—Vocational guidance—United
States—Handbooks, manuals, etc. 3. Music—Economic aspects—United
States—Handbooks, manuals, etc. I. Title

ML3790 .S74 2002
780'.68—dc21

                  2002016089

Printed in the United States of America
02 03 04 05 06   5 4 3 2 1

TABLE OF CONTENTS

Foreword by John McEuen ix

Introduction: How This Book Was Born 1
- Is this book for you? 2
- How this book is organized 2
- How to get the most from this book 3

Overview: Music, Business, and Integrity Go Hand In Hand 5
- The band story 5
- Why the media doesn't help matters 6
- Real-world success stories 7

Section One: The Art of Making Good Decisions

Chapter One: Why Are You in the Music Business? 11
- The five motivations 11
- Key concepts and definitions 12
- The profit motive: a basic issue for music people 14
- How to write a mission statement 15
- Writing it down is liberating 16

Chapter Two: How Do You Start a Music Business? 19
- The two strategic questions 19
- Risk vs. reward 20
- Why the concept of risk is so important 21
- Three key elements in any music business 21
- Three things to do before going into business 22

Chapter Three: The Bird's-Eye View of the Music Marketplace 25
- How big is the music industry? 25
- How businesses are organized for tax and legal purposes 26
- Corporate vs. independent music businesses—myths and realities 27
- Who is the customer in the music business? 27
- The two kinds of competition 28
- The threat of indirect competition 28

Chapter Four: Risk Analysis—When to Quit Your Day Job 31
- How do you feel about risk? 31
- Is anyone buying what I'm selling? 32
- Where will I get the money? 32
- Where you won't get the money 33
- Who will handle the five key aspects of the business? 34
- When to quit your day job 35

Section Two: Creating Your Essential Business Plan

Chapter Five: Why Have a Business Plan? 39
• Eight benefits of writing down your plan 39
• "It seems like a lot of work..." 43

Chapter Six: What's in a Business Plan? 45
• The memory system doesn't work 45
• The five "chapters" of your business plan .45
• A note about assumptions 46
• What do those %'s represent? 47
• Why marketing is number one 48
• How long and detailed is a business plan? 48
• Your plan's "sixth chapter": the appendix or reference section 49

Chapter Seven: The Planning Flow—From Intention to Action 51
• The right planning sequence makes a difference 51
    Plan element 1: the mission statement 51
    Plan element 2: the brand positioning statement 52
    Plan element 3: the three-year product plan 54
    Plan element 4: the operating plan 55
    Plan element 5: the daily action list 56
• Relating business planning theory to your music business 57
• How often does the plan change? 57

Section Three: Building Your Brand

Chapter Eight: Marketing and Sales Are the Keys to Your Success 61
• Competing for attention 62
• What is marketing, and how is it different from sales? 62
• The four functions of marketing 63
• The four functions of sales 64
• The seven links in the marketing chain 66

Chapter Nine: Developing Your Product Strategy 69
• Music industry products: examples of goods and services 69
• Jack of all trades, master of some... 70
• Your product mix changes over time 71
• Understanding product life cycles—the six phases 72
• How long does each phase last? 73

Chapter Ten: Your Pricing Strategy 75
• An agent's tale 75
• Charging what the market will bear—three factors 75
• The three basic pricing strategies 77
• Changing prices and revenue planning 79
• What typically happens in the music industry 80
• How to avoid pricing problems and optimize revenue 81

Chapter Eleven: Promotion, Branding, and Advertising 83
• A word about branding 83
• The promotional toolbox—ten types of tools 84
• Three key questions about your promotional strategy 91

Chapter Twelve: Your Place of Business 93
- Why place is a marketing strategy 93
  - Place dimension 1: geographical territory 93
  - Place dimension 2: channel or venue type .94
  - Place dimension 3: your workspace 95
- Your evolving place strategy 97

Chapter Thirteen: Portrait of a Salesforce 99
- Everyone plays a sales role 99
- What if I don't like the idea of sales? 100
- A word about integrity 100
- Characteristics of a great salesperson—the "three c's" 101
- The ideal sales rep 101
- What great salespeople look for in a music product 103

Chapter Fourteen: The Who, What, When, Where, Why, and How of Your Customers 107
- Understanding buyer characteristics 107
- A word about style: the Blues Brothers example 108
- Buying habits and preferences 109
- Individual vs. institutional customers 109
- What about non-viable customers? 110
- How to slice the pie 110
- Developing your target customer profile 111
- Don't let your "deal-breakers" put you out of business 112

Chapter Fifteen: Understanding Your Competition 115
- The competitive environment 115
- Identifying your direct competitors 116
- Understanding indirect competition 116
  - Exercise: Identify your top five direct and indirect competitors 117
- Why indirect competition is scarier than direct competition 118
- Competitive strengths, weaknesses, opportunities, and threats 118
- Your competitive intelligence system 119
- Your competitive database 120
- Using the seven links 120

Section Four: Applying the Fundamentals in Your Music Business

Chapter Sixteen: Doing the Numbers—Setting Realistic Goals and Objectives 125
- The importance of goals and objectives 125
- Quick review: how are goals different from objectives? 125
- Setting goals in three categories 126
  - Exercise 1: your three-year goals 128
- Turning goals into objectives: when in doubt, quantify 129
- Three key questions about setting objectives 130
- What's actually achievable? 130
- The schoolteacher paradigm 131
- How to forecast sales revenue 132
  - Exercise 2: your three-year objectives 133
- The lure of the entertainment industry—are my goals realistic? 134
- Sharing your goals with others 134
- A word of caution 135

Chapter Seventeen: Common Sense Business Lessons for the Uncommon Music World 137

- Lesson 1: When in doubt, quantify 137
- Lesson 2: The chain is only as strong as the weakest link .138
- Lesson 3: The business stuff—especially sales—is a full-time job 139
- Lesson 4: Build on strengths and delegate the weaknesses 139
- Lesson 5: Understand your customers and give them
  what they want, plus a little more 140
- Lesson 6: Understand your competitors and differentiate yourself from them 141

Chapter Eighteen: Putting It All Together 143

- Your business planning checklist 144
- Where can I get the cash I need to build my business? 145
- Frequently asked questions about business plans 145

Chapter Nineteen: Words of Encouragement— More Common Sense Lessons 149

- Lesson 1: Planning is your first and best business investment 149
- Lesson 2: No product sells itself 150
- Lesson 3: Artistic integrity and commercial viability are intrinsically compatible .151
- Lesson 4: The biggest marketing challenge is standing out from the competition . .151
- Lesson 5: It's OK to be risk-averse 152
- Applying what you've learned 153

Epilogue: Two Key Questions Revisited 154

- Three final points 154

Reference Section 155

- "Our band" business plan 156
- Worksheets and checklists 165
- Resources 183

Index 190

FOREWORD
BY JOHN McEUEN

I wish I had access to a book like this in 1966, when I signed my first major-label contract (Liberty Records, a four-album cross-collateralized deal). Had *Succeeding in Music* been around—and had I taken what I was doing with my life seriously—in the following ten years I would have made and collected about $150,000 more than I did.

When someone asks me, "How can I make it as a singer," I always advise vocal coaching. And to those who want to enter the music business, I say, either study all you can about it, or make enough money to hire a great lawyer to keep you from losing what you make. However, most musicians (or songwriters, agents, etc.) I know spend more money on health clubs and skiing lessons than on vocal coaching or business consulting. But have you ever seen a great athlete without at least one coach?

You are the business, like a farmer looking for a grocery outlet for his produce. You create things that you hope others will love, but it is your responsibility to get those creations to market. It is also your responsibility to make sure that the money earned goes to you—rest assured the companies you get involved with will be looking out for their best interests, not yours.

The music business has taken me from the Northern Lights to Japan to Georgia (both U.S.A. and Soviet Union) and to more than 5,000 shows. You can make your own rules as I and many others have, but the sooner you know their rules, the better off you will be. It is not easy, it's almost always challenging, and it's usually fun—and it can be quite profitable. But as the salesman in *The Music Man* says, "You gotta know the territory!" *Succeeding in Music* is the map of that territory. The book will give you many more hours to devote to your music and your success in it, while helping you avoid countless hours of mistakes.

A founding member of the Nitty Gritty Dirt Band, John McEuen is a musician, producer, performer, and composer whose work graces movies and television scores as well as dozens of CDs. His latest recording is Round Trip *[Chrome Records]; you can find out more about John at* **www.johnmceuen.com**.

HOW THIS BOOK WAS BORN

In the year 1998, I was invited to present a seminar on business planning at the annual convention of the International Bluegrass Music Association. My contact at IBMA explained that the audience consisted of the whole range of music people: bandleaders and musicians, agents, managers, record-label personnel, concert and festival promoters, broadcasters, songwriters, publishers, and journalists.

"Do they *want* to learn about business planning?" I asked, recalling how most of my music friends and colleagues over the years had avoided learning business fundamentals. "We don't know—we've never offered this type of seminar," was the answer. There were courses and panel discussions on getting bookings, understanding music publishing and royalties, recording and producing your own record, signing with a record label, being a better broadcaster, increasing ticket sales at festivals, and using e-mail as a promotional tool. All good stuff, but all assuming that the audience has an understanding of business fundamentals like planning, marketing, finance, and management.

Wanting to contribute to the business education of music people, I rose to the challenge and accepted the invitation. I prepared worksheets, reference materials, and slides for the overhead projector. I rehearsed. I mentally prepared for no one to show up, or for the audience response to be lukewarm. I was delighted when the room filled up and participants became eagerly engaged in the topic: "Constructing a Business Plan: Adapting Common Business Sense to the Uncommon Art of Bluegrass." I got a standing ovation at the end.

"Wow," I thought, "I've struck a nerve here." In fact, several of those original seminar attendees asked if I had written a book on the topic. Over the next year, I developed and presented additional live seminars and did a lot of research. I began to see that the *fundamentals of business* are relevant to *all* music people, regardless of industry role or music genre. That realization is what led me to write the book you are reading now. (I continue to be inspired by music audiences, and driven to bridge the gap between musical creativity and commerce through business education.)

I did Internet searches on keywords like "music business" and "busines planning." Hundreds of listings turned up. They fell into two main categories:

Category 1: The general business books, which cover the business fundamentals we will present here. The content of these books is relevant, but they do not cite music business examples, and consequently can be boring or intimidating to music people.

Category 2: The music industry books, which cover topics ranging from negotiating a recording contract to life on the road. *Succeeding in Music* provides the business foundation you need to get more out of this type of material.

In fact, this book bridges the gap between the two categories. It presents the fundamentals of business planning and marketing, which are essential for business success, but emphasizes the unique challenges facing music people.

IS THIS BOOK FOR YOU?

If you are involved in the music industry—or just thinking about becoming involved—this book is for you. That includes:

- Musicians of all kinds active in all styles of music
- Performing and non-performing songwriters and composers
- Booking agents, managers, and artist representatives
- Promoters and presenters of events, ranging from church coffeehouses to major festivals

The examples and worksheets provided in this book are geared to the group listed above. However, the fundamentals of business are relevant to *all* music people, including:

- Record producers and record-label personnel
- Music teachers and coaches
- Amateur musicians considering turning pro
- Music business students
- Partners, spouses, and parents of the above

HOW THIS BOOK IS ORGANIZED

Succeeding in Music includes four sections, a reference section, and a companion CD-ROM. It flows from the general to the specific, with key business terms and concepts defined and illustrated along the way.

- Section One: The Art of Making Good Decisions
- Section Two: Creating Your Essential Business Plan
- Section Three: Building Your Brand
- Section Four: Applying the Fundamentals in Your Music Business

The Reference Section at the end of the book and the CD-ROM provide worksheets, exercises, planning templates, a glossary, and resources for more information.

What you won't find here are gimmicks—"diet pills" and get-rich-quick schemes—or material that is readily available elsewhere (like the many excellent books on music publishing, performing, songwriting, concert promotion, etc.).

Succeeding in Music is designed to be read relatively quickly and easily. This leaves you more time to apply your new knowledge without struggling through arcane references and hyper-academic language.

HOW TO GET THE MOST FROM THIS BOOK

Everyone learns differently, so there is no single best way to enjoy this book. That said, here are suggestions for getting optimum results:

Review the table of contents. See how the book is put together and where it's going. That will help you decide which sections to focus on (and hopefully inspire you to read the whole thing).

Think about what you most want to get out of this book. Do you want to clarify basic business terms and concepts? Start writing a business plan or marketing plan? Decide if you should go into or stay in the business? Get inspired to advance to the next level? The opportunity for each of these is here.

Quickly read the whole book once before digging in to the exercises (risk analysis, mission statement, business plan, marketing plan, competitive analysis, etc.). This puts everything in perspective before you start making decisions and getting specific.

Focus on the sections that mean the most for your specific situation. For example, if you are already in the music business full-time, the "when to quit your day job" section may be irrelevant (although many have said, "I wish I knew that before I got into the business..."). If you are one of the fortunate few who already have a written business plan, focus on the practical applications and compare the concepts and templates provided here to the ones you know.

For a quick preview—and review—of the book, turn to the "Key Points in This Chapter" section at the end of each chapter. These are designed for concept reinforcement.

Plan to have a little fun. Many music people are initially put off by the business side of music. But once they get into it, they realize that business is rewarding beyond making a living—it's a different way to be creative. I've tried to capture that spirit here without sounding too corny or idealistic. In any case, keep a sense of humor and perspective throughout.

Now on with the show, and good luck!

MUSIC, BUSINESS, AND INTEGRITY GO HAND IN HAND

Music is a vital part of world culture. Music is everywhere we turn, from the background music we hear in restaurants and office buildings to live stadium shows featuring major stars. Whether music is performed live, recorded and sold as records, broadcast on radio or television, or streamed on the Internet, a team—people other than the original composer or performer—is needed to make it happen. Without the business teams of the music industry, music wouldn't reach the ears of its global audience.

Why mention this? Because so many music people—performers, songwriters, agents, managers, promoters—think that they can do it all themselves, and that they need to "sell out" or sacrifice artistic integrity to be successful financially. This unfortunate scenario seems to happen all too frequently, with negative consequences. Can you relate to the following story?

THE BAND STORY

Four musicians start a band, buy stage equipment with their life savings (and their spouse's credit cards), and soon quit their day jobs to rehearse and look for bookings. While the music sounds great, at first they have a hard time getting paid gigs. After a year or so, they are performing regularly, but still using performance revenue primarily to make equipment payments.

Another year goes by. Traveling a little bit now, the band sleeps in their van or stays with friends, unable to afford better accommodations. One band member quits due to "family pressure" (spouse wants more quality time and a "real life"). The remaining members decide to go three-piece for a while.

Even though the band has invested in making a self-produced record and is working regularly, they are only able to pay themselves a small amount of money, once in a while. Relationships start to wear thin, both in the group and with family, friends, and fans. The shows aren't fun any more, and the audience can feel it. Attendance and record sales decline. After three years of ups and downs, the band calls it quits.

You can read in all you want about the rest of the negative stuff: divorce, substance abuse, bad credit, bitterness, and disillusionment. The point is, this all-too-common scenario does not have to end this way. Here are other brief examples, relating to the same band story:

- Booking agent/manager. After a few months of finding their own bookings, the band decided it needed an agent and manager to "handle the business stuff" so the band could focus on performing and recording. They got the wife of one of the band members to handle the money and a friend to look for gigs. While these people were dedicated at first, they quickly became overwhelmed with their duties—in addition to their other jobs and family responsibilities—but kept at it out of loyalty to the band.

- Record producer. Unable to attract the interest of a professional record company, the band decided to produce its own CD. With little recording experience and less business sense, they found another former musician who had a recording studio in his basement. "Let's start our own record company. We can sell CDs at gigs and on the Internet." When the band broke up, the producer still had half of the original shipment of discs from the manufacturer and never recouped his investment in the band.

If you are a songwriter, event promoter, or play any other role in the music industry, I'm sure you can think of your own horror stories. The basic problem is this: Music people leap into the business with little or no business knowledge or experience. They think innocently that their musical chops, sweat, and sincerity are all they need to draw a crowd, sell lots of show dates and records, get rich, and be famous. Sorry, it doesn't work that way.

WHY THE MEDIA DOESN'T HELP MATTERS

The general public (that includes you and me) gets most of its music industry information from popular media, ranging from *USA Today* to *Rolling Stone* magazine to VH1's "Behind the Music" series. We hear primarily about the exceptions and the fringes of the industry, not the mainstream. For example:

- Luciano Pavarotti is reportedly paid $1 million per performance.
- Garth Brooks sells 100 million albums in ten years and retires.
- Britney Spears sells millions of records, sells out big concerts, and appears live on the Super Bowl before she is 20 years old.
- U2 sells out tours worldwide after 20 years with the same band lineup, all while campaigning valiantly for humanitarian causes.
- Bob Marley's estate accounts for a high percentage of the gross national product of Jamaica, years after his premature death.
- B.B. King wins a Grammy award and performs over 200 show dates per year at age 75.

And on and on. We also hear about all the negative extremes too. Famous musicians die of substance abuse. Personal managers and accountants are sued for taking advantage of superstars' fortunes. Record-label people go to jail for bribery and conspiracy related to radio airplay. It's tabloid journalism and it's everywhere.

Why mention all this? Here's why. Most people get their first exposure to the music industry through television, radio, and stories like the above. We have to wade through the exceptions to find examples of mainstream music business activity—the stuff that really happens day in and day out to good people who make a living and enjoy a fine career in music.

I bring this up now to assure you that this book is about business fundamentals for *all* music people and not about how to be one of the exceptions.

REAL-WORLD SUCCESS STORIES

There are an estimated two million people working in the music industry worldwide. The vast majority deal with music day in and day out and do well commercially and artistically, yet are not among the "exceptions." Don't get me wrong—anyone can potentially become a superstar, as has been proven so many times.

The point is that you can enjoy your part of the music business without enduring that constant "do or die" pressure that the media subtly inflicts upon us.

Measure your success on your own set of criteria rather than anyone else's.

Here are a few examples:

- Working musicians. Whether you are a symphony member, society bandleader, performing songwriter, touring sideman, session pro, military band member, or part of a house band at a theme park or casino, there are lots of opportunities for full-time career players.

- Agents and managers. Someone needs to get the bookings and handle the business affairs, especially those representing full-time performers.

- Record labels. Hundreds of independent record labels have proven that they do not need million-selling hit records to stay in business and make a living. Consider all the labels that have extensive catalogs that never go out of print and keep music people employed, year after year.

- Music teachers. In addition to those who work in an institutional environment (public and private schools with music programs), there are thousands of private music teachers who work in music stores and home studios.

- Music publishers, songwriters, composers, concert and event promoters, publicists, technicians—the list goes on.

There are hybrid situations too. Many music people combine activity in several of the areas mentioned above, patch it all together, and do just fine. Consider the following:

- The performing songwriter who records and earns money from royalties, record sales, and show dates

- The studio musician who tours occasionally as a sideman and teaches privately
- The managers who own record labels and handle the publishing and merchandising of the artists they represent
- The event promoters who have record labels, syndicated radio, television, and webcasting operations tied to their events

What unifies these people and the industry is a love of music and the desire to make a good living by doing what they love. Exceptions notwithstanding, music people have high integrity, positive values, and generally want to succeed. Sound corny? No—it's just like any other creative or technical field. People get into art, film, dance, theater, graphic design, photography, videography, creative writing, or scientific research for the same set of creative, financial, and personal reasons.

Here's the point: Music, business, and integrity go hand in hand. They are not mutually exclusive. Business skills are learned skills just like reading music, singing, or recording. You develop business "chops" with practice just as you do musical skills. While some people think that you have to be born with either musical talent or an aptitude for business, both can be learned—at any age.

KEY POINTS IN THIS CHAPTER

1. Music is everywhere—a vital part of world culture.

2. Many music people leap into the industry without training or experience in the business aspects of music. As in "The Band Story," this scenario can cause problems but can be prevented.

3. Most people get their music business news from the popular media: magazines, television, radio, and the Internet. We hear mainly about the exceptions of musical sucess, not the mainstream. Far more music business opportunities exist than the media report.

4. The music industry is a global business involving over two million people. There are plenty of success stories beyond the superstars and behind-the-scenes moguls, and there are many possible career paths, including hybrids.

5. Music people are unified by their love of music and desire to make a good living by doing what they love.

6. There is no need to fear "selling out" in order to be successful in music. Great music and great business go hand in hand.

7. Business problems in the music industry can be prevented. A little knowledge goes a long way.

THE ART OF MAKING GOOD DECISIONS

WHY ARE YOU IN THE MUSIC BUSINESS?

E veryone in the music business has different aspirations and motivations. Consequently, each of us is likely to answer the "why" question a little differently. Still, motivations fall into five primary categories:

THE FIVE MOTIVATIONS

1. Make a living. This ranges from "pay the bills" to "get rich." Some people are motivated primarily by money or financial need, but everyone needs some source of income. For those of us who are not independently wealthy, the prospect of making a living by doing something we love (like working in music) is attractive—a positive motivator.

2. Fulfill a dream. "I've always wanted to do something in music," or, "If only I could be in the industry doing music full-time..." Some of us want to see our name on the marquee, on records, or in the *Billboard* charts. Others aspire to business or technical support roles, but still desire a music career.

3. Create a legacy. "When I'm gone I want people to remember my music (or influence on the music industry)." Looking a little further into the future, some of us are motivated by the idea of creating a company or a body of work that takes on an identity or a "life of its own."

4. Benefit other people. "Take care of my family," or, "Inspire others..." Some of us focus on our immediate family and friends while others are driven to benefit the broader music community or society as a whole.

5. Adrenaline rush. "There's no other feeling like the energy coming from a crowd during a show." This applies whether you are onstage, backstage, or in the audience, and it can also be a positive motivator.

A possible sixth category is "all of the above." See how this sounds to you:

- "I've always wanted to do something with music that will benefit mankind— the big audience out there. If I'm successful, I'll make a good living along the way and be remembered as a positive influence on the world. When I hear the applause after one of my performances (or that of someone I'm supporting), I remember what it's all about—the music."

Sound idealistic? Maybe so, but a whole lot better than, "Oh well, I might as well get a job in the music factory because it's better than working the counter at McDonald's for minimum wage all my life…"

KEY CONCEPTS AND DEFINITIONS

Before we get into the first fundamental business planning exercise (writing a mission statement), let's establish a common vocabulary. The following words and concepts will recur throughout this book. You'll also hear them on the street or in business situations. Note: Key words and concepts are included in the Reference Section glossary and on the CD-ROM that accompanies this book.

Hobby vs. Career

Is music your hobby, or do you want to pursue it as a career? "That depends on what you mean…" Here's what I mean:

- *Hobby*: leisure activity; something done for fun
- *Career*: business activity or occupation; something done to make a living

Can you have fun while you make a living? Sure—they are not mutually exclusive, but they are different enough that it is important to make a distinction. Some music people turn a hobby into a career while others do just the opposite.

Full-Time vs. Part-Time

As in virtually every other field of endeavor, music people can work at their respective roles to varying degrees. While many devote all of their professional energy to music in some way, others do something else as a primary source of income (i.e. your "day job") and supplement that job with music. Working definitions:

- *Full-time*: geared to making 100% of financial income; implies focus and dedication
- *Part-time*: dividing time and focus among various pursuits or sources of income

Amateur vs. Professional

Just as the time factor does not refer to the quality of the results, nor does the "amateur vs. professional" concept—to a degree. In competitive sports, for example, the top amateurs can compete effectively with the top professionals. Everyone plays by the same rules and is judged according to the same performance standard. A primary difference is that amateur athletes have not "declared professional status."

How does this relate to music? Consider the definitions:

- *Amateur*: no compensation; a labor of love
- *Professional*: declared intent to work for pay; may require special training or certification by a third party

Here's the rub. Whether sports, music, astrophysics, or any other avocation or occupation, "amateur" connotes a different and lower set of performance standards than "professional." Would you hire an amateur heart surgeon? While music and entertainment are not life or death issues, the connotation carries over into music business culture.

Goals vs. Objectives

These words frequently get confused. Goals and objectives are related to one another, yet different in an important way.

- *Goal*: a desired result, often long-term; something good that you aspire to over a long period of time

- *Objective*: an aspect or subset of a goal that is specific, measurable, and achievable

Here's an example. A common goal for many people (music or otherwise) is to get rich and retire young. Getting rich and retiring young are desirable long-term results, but are not objectives.

How you reach your goals and how you measure success flows from the objectives related to the goal. For example, consider the following objective:

"I plan to have $2,000,000 in the bank by the time I am 60 years old so I can live on the interest. That will put me in a position to retire without sacrificing quality of life, and still have lots of years left to enjoy it."

This is a well-stated objective. It's specific ($2,000,000 by age 60), measurable (you can track progress from now until the objective is reached), and, for the sake of illustration, achievable.

Strategy vs. Tactics

This is another pair of frequently confused words. It's also important to make a distinction between these two, so here are the definitions:

- *Strategy*: a decision made now that affects future activities. In other words, a strategy is a thought process leading to a decision and commitment—not necessarily the behavior or work itself.

- *Tactic*: an activity designed to achieve a desired result. Tactics are the things you do to implement a strategy. Where strategy describes "what," tactics describe "how to."

Also note the connection to goals and objectives. Decisions are made (strategies) and activities are undertaken (tactics) in pursuit of desired results, both long-term (goals) and short-term (objectives).

Sound a little dry? Don't worry—I'll relate this to the music world in a moment.

Art vs. Commerce

Music is an art form. Commerce implies doing something for money. The two—art for its own sake vs. making money for its own sake—seem to be in conflict with one another. Before leaping to a conclusion, consider the following definitions:

- *Art*: human expression in sensuous form, often for its own sake. The word "expression" is very important because it implies that the motivation comes from within the artist rather than from somewhere else. More to come on this…

- *Commerce*: buying and selling of goods and services. This implies financial transactions, which further implies a profit motive.

Entertainment vs. Self-Expression

If art is human expression in sensuous form, what is entertainment? Are they related? Consider the following:

- *Entertainment*: amusement or diversion including public performances or shows. Entertainment—including music—is usually created with the needs of the audience in mind, first and foremost.

- *Self-expression*: conveyance of personal feeling, as in art. This implies that the feelings, emotions, and personal needs of the artist (composer, song-writer, performer, producer) take the highest priority. If a wide audience responds positively, that's good, but is not essential to the definition of art.

Why mention this in a business book? Because so many music people confuse the issue in their own minds and get stuck. I am not advocating one over the other, just pointing out the difference. When you write your mission statement (just ahead), you'll come back to this concept.

THE PROFIT MOTIVE: A BASIC ISSUE FOR MUSIC PEOPLE

Here's a simple formula that drives all businesses:

Revenue minus Expenses = Profit

Profit is simply the money left over after a business pays the costs of doing business. If you are a one-person music business, profit also represents the money that is available to live your life: food, housing, clothing, recreation, education, etc.

Some music people are put off by the concept of profit, feeling that the idea of having something left over after working hard for the money is evil, tacky, low-life, non-artistic, anti-art, or whatever pejorative word comes to mind. Here are my observations on this situation, gathered over a 30-year period:

- Unless you are independently wealthy (some are, but relatively few), the need to make money is a motivator for music people.

- The general public buys concert tickets, records, merchandise, and related material created by musicians and promoted by the industry. Fans vote with their pocketbooks—meaning they buy what they like and come back to the music that they enjoy on a repeated basis.

- To judge whether a specific song, record, or performance is good or bad from an artistic standpoint is largely subjective. What appeals to me may or may not appeal to you, and that's OK. Diversity keeps things interesting.

Again, what is the business point? Here it is:

Musical integrity, business integrity, and commercial success go hand in hand. You don't need to compromise musical or artistic values to make money in music. Also, simply being commercially successful does not assure positive reviews by the critics or other measures of artistic success. Remember, I'm talking about the mainstream here, not the exceptions publicized by the media.

HOW TO WRITE A MISSION STATEMENT

A mission statement answers the question, "Why are you in business?" Whether you are a self-employed individual, owner of a small music business, or in a management position in a larger firm, articulating the answer to this question is the foundation for strategic planning. Here are some guidelines:

1. Strong mission statements are usually one or two sentences long. I've seen mission statements that have gone on up to three pages of cryptic single-spaced text. Longer ones are flawed; they will not be remembered and may not emphasize essential concepts when it comes to planning and taking action.

2. Short mission statements are often supplemented by clarifying comments. These most frequently take the form of "vision statements" and "values statements." This is a good way to deal with the temptation to make your mission statement too long.

3. Vision statements describe your view of the future of the industry or market. They are part prediction, part trend analysis, part context information.

4. Values statements are your code of ethics, or the operating principles that are fundamental to your business, and unlikely to change over a long period of time. If you work alone or own the company, you can assert your own values in your music business. If you work for someone else, it is important to make sure that your personal values are reasonably aligned with those of the organization. This helps prevent problems and, more importantly, it drives the business in a positive way.

For illustration, here are excerpts from the mission, vision, and values statements in my consulting company's business plan.

Mission:

- To bridge the gap between creativity and commerce through business education.

Vision (excerpts):

- Individuals (the general public) will enjoy a gradually increasing amount of discretionary time, both on and off the job. This is an irony, as most will perceive that they have less time due to a variety of factors, including information overload and the increased rate of change.

- There is no single best way to reach a market, as there has not been a mass market for some years now. This opens the door to music-, entertainment-, and communications-based businesses that did not exist or could not flourish before.

- The relationship between creativity and commerce will stabilize eventually. Creative people (artists, musicians, engineers, entrepreneurs) will embrace the business aspects of their work in order to reach wider audiences and enjoy increased commercial success.

- As governments streamline and decentralize, businesses will increasingly support the arts with money and other resources. The two will peacefully coexist.

- To that end, we have coined a phrase: "Artistic integrity and commercial viability are intrinsically compatible." In other words, a creative or technical person does not need to "sell out" (compromise quality) in order to be financially successful.

Values (excerpts):

- Double the planning time and cut the implementation time in half. This time management rule of thumb is essential to our approach to problem solving, personal growth, and business system design.

- In any system, the chain is only as strong as the weakest link. Artistry or a great product alone cannot make up for a lack of expertise in sales, marketing, production, management, or finance. This is why it is so important to take a comprehensive view.

- Information overload can be managed and conquered. Too much information can create as many problems as not enough information.

- Every business is a people business. It is important to understand and deal with the human factors on all levels, from staff to customers to suppliers.

- Change is a prerequisite for growth. To be better implies being different; being different points to the need for change.

We'll revisit this in Chapter Seven. Also, the Reference Section and CD-ROM include a sample mission statement that can be adapted to your music business.

WRITING IT DOWN IS LIBERATING

A recurring theme in this book is "If it's not written down, it's not a plan." Sure, you have to think through the issues, and yes, you may have a good memory. Yet, there is something about the act of writing that is both clarifying and liberating.

If you are a songwriter or composer, you know what I mean. You write down sketches, notes, or fragments and put them together later. The words or notes jump off the page and make more sense the second or third time around. It's the same idea with your mission statement, and the rest of your business plan, for that matter.

The other real benefit of writing everything down is that the material can then be shared with others: your co-workers, employees, family, investors, vendors, or other stakeholders. We'll come back to this later. For now, I suggest that you take a stab at drafting your mission statement, or revising the one you currently have. Start by completing the following sentence:

We are in business to

_____

_____

_____

Congratulations! You've taken the first step in understanding the fundamentals of business and in advancing your music business to the next level.

KEY POINTS IN THIS CHAPTER

1. Everyone has their own motivations for going into the music business. These may combine the desires to make a living, fulfill a dream, create a legacy, and benefit other people.

2. It's essential to understand the difference between (a) hobby vs. career, (b) full-time vs. part-time, (c) amateur vs. professional, (d) goals vs. objectives, (e) strategy vs. tactics, (f) art vs. commerce, and (g) entertainment vs. self-expression.

3. The profit motive drives all businesses. The simple formula is *revenue minus expenses = profit*. Profit is the money left over to run your life on or reinvest in your business.

4. While some music people are uncomfortable with the ideas of money and profit, it is important to understand that they are essential to business success. Musical integrity, business integrity, and commercial success do go hand in hand.

5. Your mission statement answers the question, "Why are we in business?" and drives all other business decisions. Strong mission statements are brief—usually one or two sentences—and can be supported by additional clarifications in the form of vision and values statements.

6. Vision statements describe your view of the future of the industry or market. Values statements are your code of ethics, or the operating principles, that are fundamental to your business and unlikely to change over a long period of time.

7. Starting with a clear written statement of mission, vision, and values drives the rest of the planning process. "If it's not written down, it's not a plan."

8. If you work for or with someone else, be sure your vision and values are aligned with those of the company. This is especially important in a band or small music business situation.

CHAPTER TWO

HOW DO YOU START A MUSIC BUSINESS?

In this chapter we will outline the steps for starting a new music business. If you are already in business, I encourage you to read this section as if you were just starting out. There are likely to be suggestions to do things you've already done and done well—consider those as positive reinforcement. There are also likely to be some new items or different approaches. See how these fit with your thinking and be open to going back and filling in the gaps.

THE TWO STRATEGIC QUESTIONS

Whether starting a new business from scratch or taking your current business to the next level, there are two key questions to ask yourself.

Question 1: What do I want to accomplish?

The answers to this question tie to your motivations, goals, and objectives. Are you primarily in it for the money? Do you want to be around music and music people full-time? Do you want an outlet for your creativity?

Write down everything that comes to mind, without editing. By "without editing," I mean try to resist the temptation to think, "I'll never be able to do that..." before you write down what you want to accomplish.

Remember that at this stage, what you are envisioning and writing is just for you and there are no right or wrong answers. Also keep in mind that your goals and objectives change over time, so you'll need to ask this question on a regular basis. We'll come back to this in more detail in Chapter Sixteen. For now, we are laying the foundation for your business plan.

Question 2: How much am I willing to risk?

Any business involves risk. Risk is the possibility of danger, loss, or some other negative consequence. In any business—whether you work for yourself or someone else—your time, money, reputation, and self-esteem are at risk. Let's look at each of these briefly.

- Time. You may spend a lot of time learning new skills (musical chops, business chops), establishing relationships, and working at the music business before you achieve your financial or creative goals. How much time do you have? Can you afford to take time away from other things? Are you patient or impatient by nature?

- Money. Starting and operating a business requires cash. Do you have enough? Are you willing to put your own money at risk? If yes, how much? If no, where are you going to get the money?

- Reputation. When you operate a business, whatever you do both in your business and in your personal life is subject to public scrutiny. How do you feel about that? Are you open to praise and criticism on a regular basis, or are you more private? If you already have a string of positive accomplishments, are you willing to risk others' opinions of your work if you or your company make mistakes?

- Self-esteem. Your confidence is an asset that must be protected. I'm not referring to vanity, arrogance, or exaggerated self-importance. I am referring to the need to have a positive feeling about yourself and what you do. In any business—especially a subjective and creative field like music—your self-esteem is always at risk.

Self-esteem relates to reputation, but is really a separate concept. I've known many music people who have great reputations but are constantly criticizing themselves for what they perceive to be weaknesses or faults. They lack confidence and end up frustrating themselves and those around them as a result.

RISK VS. REWARD

A key business fundamental is the concept of *risk vs. reward*. In business, you are unlikely to get rewarded without taking some kind of risk. While it is true that the more you risk, the greater the potential reward, it is also true that the more you risk, the more you stand to lose.

Consider a lottery or raffle. You buy one lottery ticket for $1. As more people buy tickets, the pool (potential reward) gets bigger, but your chances of winning decrease.

As you buy more tickets, your chances of winning increase,
but you also have more to lose if you do not win.
As the expression goes, "The stakes get higher."

A similar risk/reward ratio exists in business. A key difference in business versus lotteries or other forms of gambling is in the amount of control that you have. In business, you control much more of what happens; the risk is more calculated. Yet, the odds of winning in business are not purely mathematical as in the lottery.

The point is this: Be willing to take risks or don't go into the music business (or any other business for that matter).

WHY THE CONCEPT OF RISK IS SO IMPORTANT

Why dwell on risk right up front? Why not get right into the rest of music business strategy? The answer comes from my own experience in the music industry. Early in my own career, I did not understand what I was risking by not having business skills when I started as a musician, and later as a booking agent. I learned the hard way and lost more time and money than I wanted to.

I also have known too many people who entered the music business without considering the risk factor. They ended up frustrated, broke, and quitting the business because they did not know what they were getting into. Some have even told me that if they *had* known, they would have gone into another field and kept music as a hobby.

Still, my motivation in this book is to inform and inspire you—not scare you off. That's why I have stressed that risk can be calculated and controlled. More on this in Chapter Four.

THREE KEY ELEMENTS IN ANY MUSIC BUSINESS

As you start or develop your business, anticipate questions that other people will ask you about what you are doing. "Other people" may be your family or friends, or may be prospective employees, partners, investors, or vendors. Below are three simple questions that define three key elements in your music business.

1. What's the business, or what is the *product*? The answer to this question is a brief description of what you do and how you add value.

- Performer: entertain audiences via live shows or records
- Songwriter or composer: create original works of music to be performed live or recorded by others
- Agent or manager: provide business services for artists
- Promoter: stage concerts, festivals, or other events where music is featured to entertain target audiences

2. What's the market or *target customer* for what you do? Who buys the product? A customer is the one who pays for your product. Products can be goods like records and T-shirts or services like a manager's advice or agent's booking and tour routing.

- Performer: customers include event promoters, record labels, and the general public or target audience
- Songwriter or composer: customers include performing and recording artists, record labels, publishing companies, and record producers
- Agent or manager: customers include performing artists, songwriters, composers, event promoters, record labels, and production companies
- Promoter and event producers: customers include venue owners, the corpo-

rate world, entertainment conglomerates, or—in the case of most independent promoters—the ticket-buying public

3. How does everyone get paid? What is the *revenue stream*? The answer here includes but goes beyond the concept of "cash, check, or credit card." You need to understand the basis for payment and earning a profit.

- Performer: soloists and group leaders are paid fees by event promoters. Sidemen are paid by the leader or business manager. Fees are negotiated in advance and widely variable. Record royalties are paid by the record company or publisher.

- Songwriter or composer: paid by publishing companies or performance rights organizations (BMI, ASCAP, SESAC, etc.). Royalty rates in most countries are standardized and regulated. Payment is based on number of records sold and number of *public performances for profit* via radio, television, film, webcasts, and other media.

- Agent or manager: paid by the artist, usually on a commission basis. This is a predetermined percentage of the artist's revenue from performances, royalties, and merchandising.

- Promoter: paid fees by corporate clients (as in producing a meeting or private party) or paid on a per-ticket basis by the general public. For large events, third party ticket agents (Ticketmaster, etc.) may be involved.

These three elements are basic business concepts that we will build upon later. Here are some additional fundamentals:

- Many music people do more than one thing. It is common for a music business to deal with multiple products, customer bases, and revenue streams.

- If you can't describe your product, you'll have a hard time selling it. More on this in Chapter Nine.

- If you don't know where the money is coming from, you'll have a hard time getting paid. This is part of the reason that music people have been burned in the past. You can prevent this problem by understanding the concept of revenue stream and how your share is determined.

THREE THINGS TO DO BEFORE GOING INTO BUSINESS

Too many music people have followed the popular "just do it" motto and gone into business without business knowledge or a business plan. While some get lucky and succeed, others suffer and fail. Success is not just a matter of musical talent or raw determination. The single most critical success factor is understanding what you are getting into—in a word, planning.

Much of the rest of this book focuses on three things to do before going into the music business:

1. **The market overview.** Understand what's going on in the music industry and how business is conducted. This is covered in Chapter Three.

2. **The feasibility study, or risk analysis.** Understand what's at risk for you and how that may have an impact on what you do in the music business. Chapter Four addresses the question, "When to quit your day job."

3. **The business plan.** Having a written business plan is essential for long-term success and is much simpler to complete than most music people think. Section Two ("Creating Your Essential Business Plan") covers the topic of constructing a business plan.

Sure, you can go into business without doing any of this, and frankly, most business people (not just *music* business people) do just that. If you are already in the music business and have experienced its ups and downs, you can likely relate to my advice. But if you are contemplating going into business, you can learn now how to prevent problems by doing the three things I've just suggested.

KEY POINTS IN THIS CHAPTER

1. Before going into business, ask yourself two key questions: (1) What do I want to accomplish? and (2) How much am I willing to risk? Write down your long-term goals and objectives early on, understanding that you will refine and revise them over time.

2. Understand the risk vs. reward principle. All business involves risk. The higher your aspirations, the more time, money, reputation, and self-esteem you risk—though it is a *calculated* risk.

3. Knowing what your product is, who your customer is, and where your revenue comes from varies according to your role in the music industry (performer, agent, etc.). Knowing how everyone gets paid is the first step in raising financial consciousness without "selling out."

4. There are three bits of homework to do before starting a business: a market overview, a risk analysis, and a business plan. These are covered in great detail in the rest of this book.

5. "Just doing it" will often get you into situations you can't control or places you don't really want to be. The most critical factor for success in any business is doing the planning work up front.

CHAPTER THREE

THE BIRD'S-EYE VIEW OF THE MUSIC MARKETPLACE

HOW BIG IS THE MUSIC INDUSTRY?

Music is big business. While the industry is fragmented and diverse, the various facets of the world of music add up quickly. Here I'm referring to the number of people employed and the resulting sales and profits, not just the cultural and entertainment value of music. While sales statistics are available for some parts of the industry (e.g., SoundScan, the point-of-sale data collection and auditing service for the record industry), no one knows exactly how many people work in the industry or how much revenue is generated annually. When concerts, record sales, publishing royalties, and music business service revenues are added together, they total in the tens of billions of dollars.

Your music business is one of tens of thousands. No one has completed a global music business census. My consulting firm estimates that over one million people are employed in the industry (part-time and full–time, in various capacities) in North America alone. Consider the following statistics:

- The American Federation of Musicians (AFM, the musicians' union) has over 115,000 members in the United States and Canada. The AFM estimates that it represents 20% of active musicians. That means that there are over 575,000 performers in North America.

- There are over 300,000 songwriters and publishers registered with ASCAP, BMI, and SESAC. In addition there are countless nonregistered songwriters and composers.

- There are over 220,000 acts (solo, duo, and bands of all kinds) that have posted songs on the music web portal MP3.com. Assuming an average of three persons for each act, that's 660,000 musicians. This roughly correlates to the AFM number, but there is likely to be many that do not overlap. The number of North American performing musicians could be as high as 1 million.

- There are over 3,700 companies listed in directories of agents, managers, and promoters. Firms vary widely in size, from a single person to over 100 people on staff. Even with an average of three people, this means that over 11,000 people are employed, just in those businesses that are listed.

As in any industry, some of the businesses in the music industry are large and complex while most are small and simple. As you might imagine, many music businesses consist of a single individual, or owner/operator, who does it all, sometimes with temporary help on a project basis. Any way you look at it, the music industry is large and dynamic. It is loaded with both opportunities and competitive challenges.

HOW BUSINESSES ARE ORGANIZED FOR TAX AND LEGAL PURPOSES

We hear a lot today about the differences between the *corporate* music and entertainment world and its relationship to the *indies* or independent music businesses. What does this mean? Why is it relevant? Here is a quick overview.

In any industry (music or otherwise), there are several ways to organize a business from a legal and tax standpoint.

- Sole proprietorship. In this type of business, one person owns the company. There may be employees, but the sole proprietor owns the assets and is responsible for the liabilities of the company. The owner is taxed on ordinary income—business revenue minus deductible business expenses. There is no stock as in corporations, so the stock cannot be traded.

- Partnership. In this type of business, more than one person owns the company, and the various owners are frequently active in the business. As with a sole proprietorship, the partners share the assets and liabilities and are taxed on their share of net company income.

- Corporation. In this type of business, there can be any number of owners (as few as one), but the company is organized according to a set of laws and tax codes that are designed to regulate larger firms. The various owners own shares of stock in the company, and that stock can be bought and sold periodically with little or no disruption to the business.

- Limited Liability Company (LLC) and Limited Liability Partnership (LLP). These are hybrid business structures in which the owners' liability for the financial and legal obligations of the company are protected by the partnership agreement, without some of the administrative detail involved in a full corporation. The concept of limited liability is attractive to investors who do not want to risk more than their individual cash investment in a given company. Basically the partners get the liability protection of a corporation with the tax advantages and the simplicity of a partnership.

- Public vs. Private. Virtually all companies listed on the various world stock exchanges (New York, London, Vancouver, Tokyo, Hong Kong, etc.) are corporations. In order to be listed (and for stock to be traded on the open market), the corporation needs to "go public," meaning that it offers shares of stock to anyone who is financially qualified to buy them. Private corporations can sell stock, but are usually closely held (relatively few shareholders) and the transactions are open to public scrutiny or regulated by the government as with public companies.

Note: Recommending one business structure or format over the other is beyond the scope of this book. Get advice from your lawyer or accountant regarding which is best for your specific situation.

CORPORATE VS. INDEPENDENT MUSIC BUSINESSES—MYTHS AND REALITIES

How does this all relate to music? First, it is valuable to understand that you have a choice of business structures when you set up your music business. Second, know that you can change the structure from time to time. Third, this may help you understand all the news and hype about the stock market.

Here's the important point for music people. "Corporate vs. Independent" is more about the structure, size, and scope of the business (as discussed above) than about the quality of the music or the integrity of the people involved. Yet, the popular media often depicts the corporate music world (the Big Five record label groups and various entertainment conglomerates) as the "bad guys" or "sellouts" and the indies as the underdogs who are "living for the music."

Note: The Big Five are BMG Entertainment, EMI Music, Sony Music Entertainment, Universal Music Group, and Warner Music Group.

Let's clear up a few myths.

Myth 1. Big is bad—they're just after the money.

Reality: Big corporate music businesses can be just as committed to their artists and to the music as small independent music businesses. The risk is higher because the cash investment is usually more. As a result, the corporate world generally focuses on safer mainstream music vs. fringe or niche music.

Myth 2. Smaller means more artist-focused and therefore better.

Reality: Small independent music businesses can be just as profit-motivated or (regrettably) insensitive to the artistic side of music as a larger business. This has more to do with the experience, skill, or personalities of the people involved than to the size or scale of the company.

In simple terms, there is no inherent connection between company size and the quality of the people or the music. The idea that "artistic integrity and commercial viability are intrinsically compatible" applies equally to the corporate and the indie worlds of music.

WHO IS THE CUSTOMER IN THE MUSIC BUSINESS?

Part of understanding the market is identifying your target customer base. In the context of drafting a market overview document, this is a critical step. In Chapter

Two we talked about the business, the market, and how everyone gets paid. We'll also get into detail in Section Three on marketing. For now, please understand two key points.

Your customer is whoever pays you directly. This is who you are responsible to in terms of adding value on a consistent basis.

The *buying public*, or the general music audience at large, is the ultimate customer for our whole industry. If the public did not buy records and concert tickets, listen to the radio, or watch television and films, there would be no need for performers, songwriters, agents, managers, promoters . . . you get the picture.

Isn't this obvious? Why mention it? This is relevant because so many music people forget where the money is coming from, and how important the customer relationship is. Which leads us to . . .

THE TWO KINDS OF COMPETITION

Any market overview and subsequent marketing plan includes a description of the competitive environment: who the competitors are and how they behave. We'll show how to do a detailed competitive analysis in Chapter Fifteen. For now, understand that there are two basic types of competition:

- *Direct Competition* = similar businesses in the same product category. Examples include other performers, songwriters, booking agents, managers, event promoters, etc.

- *Indirect Competition* = any product (goods or service) that goes after the same target customer's attention (*mindshare*) and money. Examples include not only the obvious entertainment specialists (games, cinema, sports, etc.), but alternative purchases like furniture, clothing, home improvements, computers, cars, and/or activities like vacations, hobbies, education, and leisure.

Here's an illustration: If your business is a booking agency that focuses on representing reggae arts, other reggae agencies are your direct competitors. So are any other agencies, regardless of style of music. Why? Because any agent (at least theoretically) wants to sell as many show dates as possible to music promoters. If promoters enjoy and program reggae already, it may be relatively easy to get their attention. Still, representatives of other music genres—from Appalachian to Zydeco—are also trying to sell their wares to as many promoters and fans as possible. General interest in music (as opposed to other entertainment forms) is the common thread.

THE THREAT OF INDIRECT COMPETITION

Music fans are also likely to enjoy and consume other types of entertainment: Bowling, baseball, books, magazines, movies, Super Mario, Scrabble, dancing, theater, museums, skateboarding—all of these activities take attention and cash away from music. These are examples of indirect competition from other forms of entertainment.

There's more. Put yourself in the fan's position. In addition to the multitude of music and entertainment options, you have lots of other things to do with your discretionary time and money.

> *"Should I buy a new dining room set or a new home theater system? A European vacation or a new motorcycle? Send my kid to private school or buy investment property?" Or on a smaller scale, "Should I go shopping for some new clothes, go out for a nice dinner, or go to a concert?"*

In Chapter Fifteen, we'll discuss how to understand and deal with both types of competition. For now, understand that there are two kinds, and the indirect competitors generally pose larger threats than the direct competitors.

Now that we have a perspective on the music industry, let's move on to putting your personal situation into the industry context.

KEY POINTS IN THIS CHAPTER

1. The music industry is vast, diverse, and complex. There are an estimated one million people employed (at least part-time) in the North American music industry alone, which takes in tens of billions of dollars of revenue each year.

2. You have choices for organizing your business from a legal and tax standpoint: sole proprietorship, partnership, corporation, or limited liability company. Get advice from your lawyer or accountant on which one is right for you.

3. "Corporate vs. Independent" is more about the structure, size, and scope of the business than about the quality of the music or integrity of the people involved.

4. Both corporate and indie music businesses can have musical integrity as well as profit motives. Although the media often portrays the corporate world negatively, there are more business similarities than differences between the two.

5. If you want to get paid in the music business, understand who your customer is and where the money (your cash flow) comes from.

6. The buying public is the ultimate customer for your industry. They buy the records, merchandise, and concert tickets, and provide the revenue basis for all commercial music businesses.

7. Be aware of all kinds of competition. Direct competitors offer similar products to your target customer base. Indirect competitors offer products from outside your category, but also target your customers.

8. Understanding the market is the prerequisite for your risk analysis. Once you've assessed the size and scope of the music industry, you can better determine where you want to fit in and what you are willing to risk in order to get what you want.

CHAPTER FOUR

RISK ANALYSIS—WHEN TO QUIT YOUR DAY JOB

In Chapter Two we introduced the concept of risk by asking two key questions:
1. What do I want to accomplish?
2. How much am I willing to risk?

We also identified the four things that are at risk in any business: time, money, reputation, and self-esteem. Now we will begin applying your answers to the risk questions in practical terms and equip you to answer the ultimate question: "When should I quit my day job?"

HOW DO YOU FEEL ABOUT RISK?

There are both objective and subjective aspects to answering the business questions about risk. If you are independently wealthy and have time on your hands, your perspective on what is at risk is different from the person who works a day job. Are you, or do you know anyone who is working as a retail clerk, restaurant server, cab driver, stock broker, hotel concierge, or other occupation, but really aspires to be in the music business full-time? It's a common scenario. See if you can relate to the following comments.

- "I'm working to support my music habit. When I have enough money, I'll quit to do what I really love."

- "I'm hoping to meet someone in my straight job who can invest in my music career."

- "I tried music full-time but could not make a living. I'm doing other work to pay the bills so I can still be involved in music part-time."

- "I know that the music business is risky. I owe it to my family to provide security."

- "I love the performing and songwriting but I hate the business stuff—I guess I'm not ready to take that kind of risk."

- "I love music but I'm not willing to give up my lifestyle."

Some people are comfortable with risk. Others are "risk–averse"; that is, they consciously *avoid* risk and are willing to accept lower returns as a result (remember the risk vs. reward concept). Where do you fall on the risk spectrum? Let's do a brief exercise to find out.

In the table below, simply check the boxes in each category that make the most sense to you. Remember there are no right or wrong answers. Also keep in mind that you can change your mind over time as conditions change. Here we go.

WHAT'S AT RISK	Hate to Risk Much	Willing to Risk Some	Would Risk Lots
Time			
Money			
Reputation			
Self-Esteem			

IS ANYONE BUYING WHAT I'M SELLING?

Ever wonder why a record label, agent, or manager would not sign your act? Or if you are an agent, ever wonder why an event promoter would not book the act you were pitching? The subjective willingness to take risk is a bigger factor than many music people acknowledge. Also, there are countless objective and practical reasons to buy or not buy what you are selling. Every customer has a unique set of buying criteria, including their risk tolerance. This points to the value of establishing target customer profiles as part of your overall marketing plan. (We'll cover this in detail in Chapter Fifteen.)

As you do your risk analysis, think about the question, "Is anyone buying what I'm selling?" And consider the following:

- "Is the market for what I want to do big enough to support my music business?"

- "Is there anyone else who is doing what I want to do successfully? Can I learn from them?"

- "Can I get enough facts about the size of the market to satisfy my risk tolerance?"

This last question is important in the following sense. If you have a high risk tolerance, you may be willing to leap ahead without a lot of facts and figures (like understanding how many records you need to sell or gigs you need to book to make a profit). Whatever your risk tolerance is, I suggest that you get more information on market size before quitting your day job.

WHERE WILL I GET THE MONEY?

Whether you are starting a new music business or developing your existing business, you need operating capital—cash—in order to grow. It is simply unrealistic to think that you will be paid in advance. Here's an example—typical, but idealistic and too risky:

"I'll book some gigs and use the money to buy recording equipment. Then I'll record and pre-sell enough records to pay for the manufacturing of the CD. Websites are virtually free, so I'll use the Internet to sell records and promote my act. The music is so good, it will sell itself…"

As most of you know, it does not work this way. You will need cash to start the business and then operate it over time. This money is called working capital. Here are examples of sources of cash:

- Savings. You may have a "nest egg" which you are willing to invest in your own business—cash tucked away in a savings account or "piggy bank."

- Sale of assets. You may have real estate, stocks, bonds, collectible instruments, or other securities which can be sold and turned into cash to invest in your business.

- Retirement accounts, like a 401(k) or IRA from your day job. You may be able to liquidate or borrow against the retirement fund money you have accumulated by working in a non-music occupation.

- Second mortgage. If you own your own home or other real estate, you may be able to get a home equity loan to free up additional cash.

- Credit card cash advance. Have you heard about movies that were financed by credit card debt? The interest rates are high, but it's a source of ready cash nonetheless.

- Friends and relatives. You may have the proverbial rich uncle who is willing to take a financial risk on your music career.

- Private investors. You may find individuals—other than family and friends—who are willing to invest or loan money. These people are often called "angels" or "backers."

- Reinvested profits. Once your business—whether it's your music business or another business activity you are involved in—is generating profit, you can choose to reinvest those profits as working capital.

- Banks and finance companies. The rule of thumb is this: Banks will only loan money if you can prove that you do not need it. What an irony! The point is that banks, while in the business of loaning money, have collateral and payback capacity requirements that make them more difficult to borrow from than other sources. In addition, most bankers take a dim view of music people due to bad publicity surrounding the music industry or prior bad experience with failed music businesses. Don't take it personally if your bank is not interested in loaning you money.

WHERE YOU WON'T GET THE MONEY

The following are *not* viable sources of business funding:

- Spouse's income. Many music people ask their spouse or other family members to share the risk and invest in their music businesses. This is generally not a good idea. You may ask, "Why not? My family is really supportive." This may be a tough call, but there are two primary reasons to avoid tapping the family livelihood. First, there may not be enough cash available to make a difference, even if the spirit is willing. Second—and this relates to risk of reputation and self-esteem—if anything goes wrong, you probably *don't* want to sacrifice family relationships for a few bucks that you could have gotten somewhere else.

- Part-time jobs. "But I already have a part-time job just so I can be in the music industry. Why tell me this is not a viable source of working capital?" This is another judgment call on your part, but consider this example. A person attending one of my seminars told me this: "I work a full-time (non-music) job to pay my bills and a part-time (non-music) job to support my music. I use the side money for equipment, business cards, and buying books and records." This is fine if music is your hobby. If you plan to make music your career, you simply won't have time to work one or two other jobs.

- "Bake sales and car washes." This is my expression for fund-raising activities, often associated with schools, churches, and charities. Other examples may include selling magazine subscriptions, household cleaning products, or cosmetics. Like part-time jobs, these activities are unlikely to raise enough money fast enough to make a difference.

- Illegal activities. Stealing, selling controlled substances, gambling—there are plenty of other ways to raise the money, so avoid nefarious methods.

WHO WILL HANDLE THE FIVE KEY ASPECTS OF THE BUSINESS?

Any business—music or otherwise—has five key elements:

Product development. This involves getting the product (goods or services) ready to offer to your target customer base. An obvious music example is the need to rehearse before going on stage or in the studio. Getting your musical chops together is an example of product development. If you are an agent, manager, or promoter, you need to identify and sign acts. That process—before anything is sold—represents product development.

Product delivery. Back to the performer example. Once you've rehearsed and have booked performance dates, you need to show up and do the work. If you are a songwriter, once you've written a song, you need to deliver it to your publisher or the artist you are pitching. Promoters deliver the *product* (live entertainment) on the day of the show.

Sales and marketing. Regardless of what the product is, someone needs to handle the sales and marketing. We'll devote quite a bit of this book to this subject in Section Three ("Building Your Brand").

Accounting and finance. Someone needs to keep track of the money, pay the bills, raise extra working capital when needed, file the tax returns, and keep an eye on the eventual profits of your business.

Management. Any business—even a one-person business—needs to be managed. Beyond just handling administration and operations (information systems, workplace facilities, human resources), management has four key responsibilities. They are (1) planning, (2) organizing, (3) motivating, and (4) controlling. The larger your business, the more likely that these four essential functions take up 100% of someone's time.

Many music people try to do it all. Some are content and successful, others end up getting frustrated. Does this sound familiar? "I'm a songwriter and performer. I handle my own bookings and promotion. I record in my home studio and make discs to order on my CD recorder. When I get a record order, I pack it up, enclose a personal thank-you note, and take the package to the post office. I balance my own checkbook, and troubleshoot my computer when it goes down."

I admire these people. In fact I've known quite a few over the years. I've also known many music people who want to focus on what they love to do and what they do best. There is no right or best way. As a practical matter, no single person can do everything effectively, especially as the business grows.

Think about the music people that you admire or emulate. Do they do everything themselves? Relatively few career performers or recording artists handle their own booking (sales), management, and accounting. Agents and managers are seldom performers. Excellence requires full-time focus on what you do best.

Here's the point: Someone needs to take care of each of the five essential elements of your music business. Is it you for all five, or can you focus on one or two? What are you best suited for? What feels right? How can you make the best contribution? How can you have the most fun along the way?

Addressing these questions is part of your risk analysis. It is human nature to be willing to take more risk in the areas where you are more skilled and confident. You may also be more comfortable sharing the risk with others who understand these concepts and are willing to contribute their part to complement yours. Now, on to the important question.

WHEN TO QUIT YOUR DAY JOB

If you are doing something other than music to make a living but would like to focus on music full-time, this is *the* important question. If you are already doing music full-time, the conditions below are still valuable to put into perspective.

There are three conditions to be met before you can "quit your day job" with confidence:

1. You have a business plan, written down and ready to share with others. This is the subject of Section Two ("Creating Your Essential Business Plan") of this book (you're almost there!).

2. You have funding to cover both business and personal expenses for at least one year (once you have drafted your business plan, you'll know how much money is enough). Why one year? Because less than a year is not long enough to work through your plan in most cases. You are likely to generate revenue in much less than a year, but having the financial support up front provides the confidence to move ahead and the cash in case a problem or opportunity arises.

3. You are comfortable taking the risk. We've spent a lot of time in this chapter talking about the various kinds of risk. Some people handle risk easily, others don't. There is no rule on how much risk to take, so don't feel that one or the other is the best way. Just determine how much risk *you* are willing to take and proceed from there.

It helps a lot to have family and friends who are comfortable with your music business idea, too. Having that emotional support is likely to make things go a lot easier, especially on the home front.

If any of the three conditions are not met, you are probably not ready to quit your day job. You may say, "I'm comfortable with the risk and I have some money, so I don't need a business plan." Or, "I've got a business plan, so I'll use it to raise the money." Or, "I'm already in the business, I'll finance it from cash flow, and I'll get used to this sick empty feeling in my stomach, wondering how I'm going to pay rent and phone bills."

I view all of these as "eager rationalizations." The eager part is very positive. You want to do it because music is so important to you. Beware of overrationalization, however. Why did you buy this book? How did you get to this point? It is probably because you want to get ahead by some means other than trial and error.

KEY POINTS IN THIS CHAPTER

1. Be comfortable with risk, or else don't take risks. There is no best way or single right answer to the question of how much risk to take.

2. Understanding what's involved when going into business is essential to understanding the risk factor. Many music people are unaware of what it takes to operate a music business and leap in prematurely.

3. Understand the market for your music product before developing your business further. Ask the question, "Is anyone buying what I'm selling?"

4. Any music business requires working capital—cash—in order to operate and grow. There are many sources of cash other than the revenue generated by the business. Some are better than others when it comes to assessing both financial and emotional risk.

5. Savings, retirement accounts, sale of assets, second mortgages, credit card advances, and private investors are among the viable sources of working capital. Examples of nonviable sources of cash include spouse's income, part-time jobs, and "bake sales and car washes."

6. Any music business has five key elements: (1) product development, (2) product delivery, (3) sales and marketing, (4) accounting and finance, and (5) management. Be confident that you do not necessarily need expertise in all five areas, which points to the idea of building your team.

7. Don't quit your day job prematurely. To focus on your music business full-time, you must: (1) have a written business plan, (2) have enough cash to cover business and personal expenses for a minimum of one year, and (3) be comfortable taking risks. If one of these three conditions is not met, you are not ready to go into music full-time.

8. Beware of "eager rationalizations" or the tendency to be idealistic. Having a written business plan is the first step towards quitting your day job and the topic of the next section of this book.

CREATING YOUR ESSENTIAL BUSINESS PLAN

"Fail to plan, plan to fail."—business truism

CHAPTER FIVE

WHY HAVE A BUSINESS PLAN

A business plan is a document which guides any business toward its future goals and objectives. Two key words there: document and future. The word "document" implies that the contents of the plan are written down. The word "future" implies that the business is moving in a forward direction and eager to make progress over time.

Sound simple? It is. Then why do so few businesses in any field—music or otherwise—have written business plans? While most businesses have some sort of record-keeping system and a financial budget, only about 5% have a comprehensive plan. Many of my consulting firm's clients over the years have initially said, "Sure I have a business plan. It's all right up here" (pointing to their head, indicating that the plan is etched in their memory).

Yikes! How do you share such a plan with staff, customers, vendors, or investors—telepathy? What if the boss—which could be you—ends up unable to share the information? Even the most creative ideas and best-laid plans need to be written down. Consider the following scenarios:

- The business founder or leader loses interest and goes on to another job or project.
- The lead person dies or becomes unable to talk or write, let alone work.
- The ideas upon which the business is based are wrong, outdated, or incomplete.
- A dispute arises over who had an idea first.
- Key people like employees or partners (which could be band members, support staff, or investors) lose interest and move on.

I've seen all of these happen at one time or another, and the results are not pretty. People end up losing—you guessed it—time, money, reputation, and self-esteem. Problems could have been anticipated and prevented, but they weren't.

EIGHT BENEFITS OF WRITING DOWN YOUR PLAN

Key point: A business plan is the single most valuable tool of any business. Here are eight reasons or benefits for not only having a business plan, but writing it down.

Benefit 1: Road Map

Your business plan is your road map to the future. Consider this analogy:

You want to visit a city you've never been to before, and you plan to drive there in your car. You look at a road map and discover that there are several routes to your destination. One is the most direct—the fastest via interstate highway, but a little boring. Another is the scenic route. It takes a little longer, but interesting sights are along the way. A third route goes along county highways most of the way and is pretty fast, but allows you to get a feel for the local culture as you travel.

In business, multiple routes also lead to your business goals and objectives. Some are faster but more costly. Others leave open the possibility for "sight-seeing," or experimenting, as new ideas or opportunities crop up. The map (your plan) shows you the options and provides a reference to fall back on if you get lost or encounter unexpected "road construction" along the way.

Benefit 2: Measuring Stick

There's a business axiom that states:

"What gets measured, gets done." Remember the definition of an objective? "An aspect of a goal which is specific, measurable, and achievable."

Your business plan includes goals and objectives, financial and otherwise. Those objectives are plotted on a timeline or list of milestones (another road-map reference). The plan allows you to see how you are doing relative to your objectives at any point in time. Chapter Sixteen deals with how to set realistic goals and objectives. For now, understand the value of having a written reference for measuring your success.

Benefit 3: Opportunity Management Tool

Most music businesses have more opportunities than they can handle. There are more possible show dates to play or promote, acts to book and manage, or songs to write and produce than any one business has the capacity or expertise to accommodate. This applies to the big corporate companies as well as the small independent ones. The business buzzword here is "capacity." You may have ambition and opportunity, but if the capacity, rationale, or capability is not there, the results may be less than desirable.

Your business plan is an opportunity management tool. If the next hot creative idea is within the scope of your plan, you can address it with energy and confidence. If not, you can pass or refer the opportunity to someone else, also with confidence. By thinking of your plan in this way, you'll be less likely to take bookings or sign artists who present themselves as available, but don't make sense or feel right. You also have a polite way to turn down the marginal opportunities. It's better to say, "Sounds good, but it's outside the scope of our business," than to get involved in the wrong project and regret it later.

Benefit 4: Stress Management Tool

Everyone in business is under stress to some degree. Stress is a demand on your mental and physical energy. We'll discuss two types of stress: distress and eustress. Distress is the negative kind, which results from too many things to do in too short a period of time with too few resources. Sound familiar? You've probably encountered the uneasy feelings that come from information overload, financial concerns, deadlines, or uncertainties inherent in your job or family situation.

Eustress is the good feeling that comes from having a creative idea that energizes you. Think about when you were a kid and looked forward to a birthday party, family vacation, or a favorite sport or hobby (maybe music?) that you loved doing. You stayed up all night with thoughts of the positive activity spinning in your head. Have you ever had that type of feeling about your music career? I hope so. Songwriters and composers can relate to this easily, but so can any other music person who has a good idea and opportunities for success.

Consider the stress on yourself and your employees as the business grows. Much energy, time, and money are wasted in the business world because the people simply don't know what to do at any given time. Your business plan helps everyone answer the following question:

"Am I doing the right thing for my business, right now?"

When you know the answer is yes, you proceed with higher confidence and lower stress.

Your business plan is a terrific stress management tool. It helps you anticipate and prevent problems. It provides the context information and contingencies for dealing with unanticipated challenges. It helps you focus your creative energy on your goals and objectives. All of these activities help you lower or manage the normal stress that comes with being in the music business.

Benefit 5: Catalyst for Your Best Work

"But I want to be open to anything. I don't want to feel encumbered by a business plan. That's why I'm in a creative field like music…"

Consider the great graphic artists. I enjoy visiting art museums, and I am particularly fascinated by artists' sketches and notes that led to the great paintings and sculpture. From Michelangelo and da Vinci, to Rembrandt and Van Gogh, to Picasso and Hopper, fine artists created their own "business plans" for their major works in the form of sketches and studies. How does the analogy work? When you have an idea of what you want the finished work to look like and have written it down, you can channel your creative energy toward achieving the best possible results. It's likely that your creativity will be unlocked rather than stifled!

Benefit 6: Competitive Weapon

Your business plan helps you deal with your competitors—both direct and indirect. As I've noted, only about 5% of all businesses have written plans. In the music industry and other creative and technical fields that number is probably less, although no hard statistics exist. You may ask, "If that's the case, why bother? My competitors are no better off than I am."

Here are two key points: First, a higher percentage of your indirect competitors (the big scary ones from outside of the music industry) are likely to have business plans. That puts them at an advantage over you. Second, 95% or more of your direct competitors are unlikely to have a business plan. That puts you at an advantage over them.

In either scenario, your business plan is a competitive weapon. It helps you defend your business from competitive threats at the same time that you seize competitive opportunities that are consistent with your long-term goals and objectives.

Benefit 7: Fund-raising Tool

Ever try to borrow money for anything? Whether you are asking a friend for some spot cash until payday or seeking a mortgage on a new home from a bank, you can anticipate two questions:

- What are you going to do with the money?
- When and how are you going to pay it back?

Even if you are using your own savings or a credit card cash advance to finance your next stage of growth, you will need to ask yourself these same questions. Your business plan points to the answers.

While some angel investors or banks will provide small amounts of money having received minimal details, the process gets tougher as the stakes get higher. Anticipating this, your business plan is an essential fund-raising tool.

Benefit 8: Team-Building Tool

How do you find people with complementary skills to round out your team? What are they going to do once you find them? What's the pay and benefit package? Your business plan includes the answers to these questions and more.

Once your team is put together, the plan serves as a guide (road map, measuring stick, etc.) for everyone involved, not just the owners and investors. Employees—from band members to accounting clerks—feel like they are "on board" when they have access to the company's mission, vision, values, operating policies and procedures, goals, and objectives. Your business plan is your best team-building tool.

"IT SEEMS LIKE A LOT OF WORK..."

You may be thinking, "OK, you've presented a logical argument for constructing a written business plan, but it still seems like a lot of work. Is it *really* worth it?"

Once again, I'll go back to the concept of risk vs. reward. If you are comfortable putting everything on the line with minimal planning, that's your decision. Your family, staff, partners, investors, and customers are probably more risk-averse than you are. In that case, do it for them, and enjoy the extra benefits yourself.

You'll probably also find out that the planning process can be creative, fun, and invigorating. Once your plan is written, you'll look back and wonder what you did without it. But don't just take my word for it—get started.

KEY POINTS IN THIS CHAPTER

1. "Fail to plan, plan to fail." This business truism points to the need to have a plan for any business, large or small.

2. A business plan is a document that guides any business toward its future goals and objectives. Your plan keeps you in control, helping you anticipate rather than react to opportunities and threats.

3. Many businesses think they have a plan because the owner or key executives have the best interests of the company in mind. That's nice, but if it's not written down, it's not a plan.

4. There are eight compelling benefits to having a written business plan: (1) road map, (2) measuring stick, (3) opportunity management tool, (4) stress management tool, (5) catalyst for your best work, (6) competitive weapon, (7) fund-raising tool, and (8) team-building tool.

5. Staff, vendors, partners, investors, and customers respond positively when you have a business plan. The benefits more than justify the effort required to create the plan.

6. The planning process is invigorating and can be fun.

CHAPTER SIX

WHAT'S IN A BUSINESS PLAN?

In this chapter we'll provide the details on the various elements of a business plan. To get started, here's our working definition:

A business plan is a written system of documents that puts your business and its market environment in context over the course of the next several years. It describes (1) what you are going to do, (2) how you are going to do it, and (3) the consequences.

You may be thinking, "I know the answers to those questions already." Good! Now is the time to write them down.

Note: This chapter gives a brief overview of what's in a business plan so you can quickly see how the parts fit together in a systematic way. We'll break down each part in more detail in subsequent chapters. See the Reference Section of this book or the CD-ROM for definitions of any business terms that may be new to you and for a sample business plan illustrating the concepts presented here. Also remember that even if you work alone, think of yourself as a "company" for planning purposes.

THE MEMORY SYSTEM DOESN'T WORK

A recurring theme in this book is: "If it's not written down, it's not a plan." Here's why the "memory system" of business planning doesn't work.

- No one person has all the answers, let alone the ability to remember them.

- Your memory can't always be consulted on demand, such as when you are on vacation and a staff person back home needs to make an operating decision.

- Even if you are a single-person business, it's inefficient to communicate all the details verbally to family, friends, vendors, co-workers, bankers, investors, or anyone else who needs to know. They want it written down.

THE FIVE "CHAPTERS" OF YOUR BUSINESS PLAN

Before we talk about length and format, let's first understand the content of a business plan.

A comprehensive plan has five sections or "chapters":

Chapter 1: Description of your company, business, and place in the industry (15%)

Briefly describe what business you are in, who your customers are (category vs. individual names), a summary history of your activities, and what role you play in the global music and entertainment industry.

Chapter 2: Description of products (goods and services) (15%)

Go into more detail here about the specific things you do, merchandise you sell, or services you provide. Discuss key features and customer benefits, along with your competitive advantages.

Chapter 3: Market overview and marketing strategy (35%)

Describe the size and growth of your specific market. Keep in mind the big picture, as we discussed in Chapter Three of this book. Talk about target market segments, the competitive environment, your promotion strategy, geographical territory and place of doing business, channels of distribution, and salesforce. Include profiles of target buyers and examples of key current customers. Tie the promotion strategy to your three-year goals and objectives.

Chapter 4: Management team and organizational overview (25%)

Here's your chance to relate your professional experience and why you are qualified to do what you are doing. If the business includes more than one person, include brief biographies of the current management team and a description of staff, consultants, and vendors. Show the reporting structure and how the organization will change over time as the company grows. Include brief descriptions of positions on your team that have not been filled yet, but are planned.

Chapter 5: Financial summary (10%)

Provide details on sales revenue, expenses by category, capitalization, cash flows, and income forecast. Just show the financial highlights and key financial assumptions—you'll include budgets and pro forma income statements in the appendix to the plan.

A NOTE ABOUT ASSUMPTIONS

The word "assumption" comes up regularly in business. You may have heard the old expression, "Never assume anything." This is generally good wisdom, but the slogan is an abbreviation of something with a slightly different meaning: "Never assume that anything is 100% committed and unchangeable."

In a business context, here is the definition of the word assumption that we use:

Assumption: the answer to the question, "How did you get the numbers?"

In business, you need to make plans based on a set of assumptions. There are market assumptions, financial assumptions, staffing assumptions, and scheduling assumptions. How well you plan and how well you succeed are entirely dependent on how reasonable and how accurate your business assumptions are.

Some business people—not just music people—have a hard time writing down assumptions. "I won't write it down if I don't know for sure; I don't want to make a commitment I can't keep." A noble philosophy, but it just doesn't work most of the time. Here are examples of potentially faulty assumptions that might not have been made if they had been written down.

- "I'll move to the city, get discovered, get a record contract, tour, and get rich."

- "All I have to do to get more bookings is hire a manager."

- "All I need to do to make more money is play more gigs." (Or sell more records, write more songs, sell more tickets, represent more acts, etc.)

- "There's no way I can make a living in music, so I'll just keep working these three part-time jobs to support my music habit."

- "No one is interested in my style of music."

The list can go on and on. But making assumptions and then backing them up with answers to the questions posed in this book are essential to both the business planning process and to long-term success in music.

WHAT DO THOSE %'s REPRESENT?

Back to the contents of your business plan. Did you notice those percentages shown after each chapter description? What do they signify? Where do they come from?

Chapter 1: Company, business, and industry overview (15%)

Chapter 2: Products overview (15%)

Chapter 3: Market overview and marketing strategy (35%)

Chapter 4: Management team and organizational overview (25%)

Chapter 5: Financial summary (10%)

The percentages indicate the relative weight or importance of each section. They add up to 100%, and all are essential to your plan. Here they are again, ranked in order of importance:

Chapter 3: Market overview and marketing strategy (35%)

Chapter 4: Management team and organizational overview (25%)

Chapter 1: Company, business, and industry overview (15%)

Chapter 2: Products overview (15%)

Chapter 5: Financial summary (10%)

The ranking system comes from the investment world, the hard-core business people. In this case, the guidelines are those provided by the Los Angeles Economic Development Council (LAEDC), a city office that assists inventors or entrepreneurs who are seeking financing or investment capital. The LAEDC screens dozens to hundreds of business plans each year and provides this weighting scale to assist small businesses in making their presentations to investment bankers, venture capitalists, private angel investors, and other financial organizations or sources of cash.

WHY MARKETING IS NUMBER ONE

When I first came across this set of planning guidelines years ago, I thought to myself, "Wow! I would think that financial people would rank the financial component of my business plan as the highest in importance." Seems logical, but the reality is that you can make the "financials"—sales revenue, expenses, profits, etc.—look any way you want on paper. Financial people know that. While the numbers are important (10% of your plan), the other aspects of the plan are more important! You must be able to answer questions.

"How did you get the numbers?" or "What are you going to do to achieve your sales targets?" is actually more important than the numbers themselves.

Look at the percentages noted above one more time. What's number one in ranking? Market overview and marketing strategy. Other than creating an excellent product, competing for attention—marketing—is the biggest business challenge facing any music business. Savvy business people—including financial experts—know this. That's why we devote Section Three ("Building Your Brand") of this book to marketing and sales.

HOW LONG AND DETAILED IS A BUSINESS PLAN?

Let's go back to your own business plan, whether you are going to show it to financial people or not. The first inclination for most people drafting a business plan is to think, "More is better—let's get all the facts and impress our staff or financial backers with lots of details." This is part right and part wrong.

The correct part is to do your homework and have facts available. The incorrect part is to assume that anyone other than yourself will actually read the proverbial novel-length business plan, with reams of text, graphs, charts, circles and arrows, clippings, and other support materials. This mistaken assumption is a big reason why such a high percentage of all businesses don't have a written plan. What an irony!

Here's the reality, followed by a suggestion. First, remember that the plan is primarily for you, so you decide how much detail you need. If you are developing an organization or seeking financing, you may need more than one version of the plan. This is analogous to songs that are recorded multiple ways depending on how they are going to be used (radio mix, club mix, album mix, live mix). The core content is the same but the packaging is different depending on the target audience.

"So, where do I start?" A solid business plan includes the following:

1. Fifteen to twenty pages of text that follow the five-chapter outline above

2. Financial schedules, including detailed monthly budgets for the next year and summary budgets for two more years

3. Reference material that supports the text and the financials

We'll go into more detail on how to put the plan document together in Chapter Sixteen.

YOUR PLAN'S "SIXTH CHAPTER": THE APPENDIX OR REFERENCE SECTION

It's human nature to procrastinate reading or writing long, detailed documents. You can help everyone by breaking your plan down into bite-sized chunks. To keep the text portion of the plan brief and concise, put the backup information in an appendix or Reference Section. Note: The details are important, but it's the essence of those details that comprise the essence of your plan.

Here are examples of items that can be included in the Reference Section:

- Organizational chart
- Job descriptions and consultant bios
- Information policy
- Master client history spreadsheet ranked by total sales
- Product plan spreadsheet
- Historical financial data
- Customer profiles and target customer criteria
- Sample promotion materials, press clippings, awards, website content
- Employee handbook including company policies and benefits
- Market research reports and statistics
- Detailed profiles of competitors

Seem like a lot? It is, but don't worry. You're about to learn how to gather the information for your business plan in an organized way.

KEY POINTS IN THIS CHAPTER

1. A business plan is a written system of documents that describes (1) what you are going to do, (2) how you are going to do it, and (3) the consequences.

2. "If it's not written down, it's not a plan." Having the plan organized and available to others is powerful and essential for business success.

3. A business plan has five key "chapters":
   Chapter 1: Company, business, and industry overview (15%)
   Chapter 2: Products overview (15%)
   Chapter 3: Market overview and marketing strategy (35%)
   Chapter 4: Management team and organizational overview (25%)
   Chapter 5: Financial summary (10%)

4. The market overview and marketing strategy section carries the most weight, especially with financial people or investors.

5. Assumptions answer the question, "How did you get the numbers?" There are market assumptions, financial assumptions, staffing assumptions, and scheduling assumptions. All need to be written into the business plan.

6. Less is more—be brief, concise, and accurate. Good, readable business plans consist of about 15-20 pages of text plus detailed financial schedules and reference information.

7. Put the backup details in the appendix or Reference Section, or "sixth chapter," of your plan. Examples range from organizational charts to sample promotion materials to market research information.

CHAPTER SEVEN

THE PLANNING FLOW— FROM INTENTION TO ACTION

THE RIGHT PLANNING SEQUENCE MAKES A DIFFERENCE

We've discussed the contents of your business plan. Now we'll help you create a *planning flow*—doing things in the right sequence to optimize results. We'll present the perfect-world scenario first, then provide tips on dealing with the reality that it's not a perfect world, and that many music businesses are already up and running, with or without a business plan.

Planning in the right sequence can prevent problems and help preserve artistic integrity. That's a strong statement. Consider a scenario in which you are starting your business from scratch and you have time to do the planning before leaping into the market. Here is the recommended planning flowchart.

Plan Element	How Long	Essential Components
1. Mission statement	Indefinite	Purpose, vision, and values
2. Brand positioning statement	Indefinite	Goals; long-term objectives
3. Product plan	2–5 years	Strategy
4. Detailed operating plan	1–2 years	Tactics; short-term objectives
5. Daily action list	Daily	Implementation

PLAN ELEMENT 1: THE MISSION STATEMENT

All business planning—and the best business plan—flows from concise statements of mission, vision, and values. We touched on this in chapter one. Remember the exercise where you answered the "why are we in business?" question? Your vision of the future market? Your personal and company values?

As the flowchart on the previous page indicates, mission statements are designed to last indefinitely. When you are tempted to change your mission statement (this will happen periodically), take a step back and see if you are reacting to an unforeseen opportunity or problem, or actually considering another business with a separate mission. Once you pinch yourself and see what's really going on, you are likely to keep your mission intact and adapt other elements of the plan rather than changing your mission to reflect the moment.

PLAN ELEMENT 2: THE BRAND POSITIONING STATEMENT

Once you've articulated your mission statement, the next element in the planning flow is the *brand positioning statement*. Like the mission, the position that you plan to develop for your brand (even if the "brand" is you) is likely to last a long time unless business or personal conditions change substantially. Many music businesses get into trouble by changing strategic direction whimsically and frequently. Your brand positioning statement is a key tool in preventing that problem and in focusing your business efforts.

Your brand positioning statement is a one-page document that answers the following four questions:

1. What business are we in? (what you do)
2. Who are our customers? (where the money changes hands)
3. What makes us special? (especially relative to competitors)
4. What's in it for everybody? (you, your customers, employees, vendors, the community)

Below is a sample brand positioning statement for a booking agency. You can adapt this example for other types of music businesses using the templates included in the Reference Section of this book and on the CD-ROM.

The Acme Agency is in the business of providing artist representation services on a commission basis. We sell performance dates and related musical services, administer contracts, assist with general artist promotion, and coordinate itineraries. Our clients include artist management companies, independent bands, and performing songwriters. We focus on festivals, fairs, college campuses, showcase clubs, and municipal events in North America. We are allied with associate agencies for co-representation in Europe.

Our clients are motivated by a combination of needs, including:

1. The need for steady bookings in quality venues

2. The need to develop and protect market share in key entertainment segments

3. The need to branch out into new markets

4. The need to coordinate travel and logistics to optimize health and costs

5. The need to coordinate live performances with publicity and broadcast opportunities

We provide our clients with a special blend of music industry knowledge, sales, marketing, and management experience, and the ability to work with a wide range of personal and organizational styles. We consistently exceed both client expectations and competitive offerings in the following areas:

- Quality of results. We secure bookings in quality venues for optimal performance fees.

- Clarity and objectivity. We identify performance opportunities and problems efficiently and communicate them accurately to our artist and manager clients. Maintaining an independent viewpoint, we provide a clear picture of the current situation and recommend action accordingly.

- Adaptability and flexibility. We integrate easily within each client's unique music business environment. We are versatile and work comfortably in most business situations.

- Attention to detail. We know that the little things count. We take pride in our thoroughness and accuracy in contracting, communication, and follow-up.

- Timeliness and accountability. We seize opportunities as they arise and stay in constant touch with our clients. We work within itinerary routing and financial guidelines provided by the artist or manager.

Clients regard The Acme Agency as a special business resource. We play the roles of sales agent, marketing department, and tour manager—one, two, or all three depending on the situation. Artist, venue, and management relationships are long-term.

We are acknowledged by the music industry—clients and competitors alike—as a leading agency, known for quality artists and fair dealing. Together, we share goals, creative ideas, frustrations, industry perspectives, and rewards. Our long-term success is measured in terms of our artists' ability to work consistently, profitably, and artistically.

In the above example do you see how all four questions were answered? If The Acme Agency was your business (or your agent for that matter) how would you feel? What have we accomplished?

Once again, you may be thinking, "I know all that. Why should I write it down?" For the answer to the "why write it down" question, see chapter five. It's more likely that you may be thinking, "I've never really answered these questions in a concise way. It looks good on paper—almost too good to be true." That's the more typical response. When you have a written brand positioning statement, you have a tool which can be used in the following ways:

- Foundation for your marketing plan. By thinking through the four questions early in the planning process, your marketing plan will be easier to construct.

- Basis for evaluating opportunities. As opportunities arise—booking possibilities, recording offers, publishing deals, or whatever is relevant to your business—you can check them against your brand positioning statement as well as your mission. If they fit, keep going; if not, you can respectfully decline with a clear conscience and no hard feelings.

- Elements of company promotion materials. As you develop materials (sales literature, publicity, advertising, website content, and even album liner notes), you can use the brand positioning statement to be sure that your public message is consistent with your plan. It helps keep you in control of the marketing process.

- An intended target. Since you are drafting the positioning statement early in the planning process, it sets the tone and provides a foundation for your long-term goals and objectives. It's OK if it sounds a little idealistic or motivational.

The "Elevator Test"

One of the ways to be sure that your brand positioning statement does not ramble on too long is to apply the elevator test. Imagine that you get on an elevator in a tall building with someone you have never met. That person asks the question, "What do you do?" You only have the time that it takes to go up or down about ten floors in the elevator, but you want to make a good first impression.

Rather than fumble or respond with the euphemistic "it's a long story..." or "I wear many hats..." type of answer, go to your brand positioning statement in your mind and answer the first two questions:

- "I'm in the music business as a (fill in your role here)..."

- "My customers are (fill in your target customer profile here)..."

This clarifying experience helps you answer the key questions concisely and in language that does not presuppose music industry knowledge on the part of the person asking the question. While you may never have a stranger ask you for this information in an elevator, the following types of people are likely to ask at some point.

- Prospective customers, employees, and vendors

- Your banker, accountant, or lawyer

- Your parents, friends, and family

- People you meet at parties, weddings, or other events (like your class reunion)

A properly articulated brand positioning statement is a key element in your business plan and a tool that has multiple applications. You are better off thinking through the answers to the four questions *early* in the planning flow rather than later or not at all.

PLAN ELEMENT 3: THE THREE-YEAR PRODUCT PLAN

Understanding your product and where it is going over the next three years is the next element in the planning flow. First, a quick definition of "product":

● Your product is the result of your labor and what your customers pay for.

There are two broad categories of products: goods and services. Goods are tangible; services are intangible. Much of the music industry is based on *services as products*. Consider the chart below.

Your Industry Role	Product Example	Goods	Services
Performing musician	Live performances		x
Booking agent	Secure bookings		x
Manager	Provide management services		x
Record label	Recorded music (CD's, etc.)	x	
Event promoter	Entertainment experiences		x
Songwriter	Original compositions		x
Music teacher	Learning experiences		x
Merchandiser	T-shirts, jackets, identity items	x	
Publisher	Song promotion and royalty administration		x

We'll expand on this theme in chapter nine when we discuss product strategy in the context of your comprehensive marketing plan. For now, the point is to understand that your long-term product strategy drives the tactical aspects of the business plan. For example, you simply can't set sales revenue objectives or plan staffing and promotional techniques if you do not know what products you plan to offer.

PLAN ELEMENT 4: THE OPERATING PLAN

Once you've got the first three elements—mission, brand positioning statement, and product strategy—you are in a position to create an *operating plan*. This is the part of the plan that most people—music or otherwise—think of when they think of a business plan. Let's make a distinction here. Remember the definition of strategy vs. tactics? A strategy is a decision; a tactic is a method. In a business plan, *both* strategies and tactics are articulated.

Many businesses have a sales forecast and expense budget, both key elements of a tactical operating plan. Relatively few businesses frame the numbers with the strategies and operating assumptions that really make a good plan come to life. Here are the key elements of the tactical operating plan:

1. **Detailed revenue forecast.** Revenue = units sold x average selling price. If you are selling records on a wholesale basis or calculating song royalties, the process is pretty simple. If you perform live in multiple types of venues at different prices, it's a little more complicated. If you do more than one thing—perform, write songs, and sell your own records—you will need a line item in your revenue forecast for each item. We'll come back to this in Chapter Sixteen.

2. **Marketing plan.** The seven elements of the marketing plan will be covered in detail in Section Three ("Building Your Brand").

3. **Budgets and pro forma financials.** These are the hard-core financial schedules, related to both income (see the revenue forecast) and expenses in all areas. The words "pro forma" come from Latin and imply that portions of the material are hypothetical (future) as opposed to actual (real history). Examples of financial materials include departmental or project expense budgets, profit and loss (*P&L*) or income statements, and balance sheets. See definitions in the glossary.

4. **Organization plan.** This includes a listing of each staff position, the reporting structure (best illustrated in a graphic organizational chart), job descriptions for each position, and a description of employee benefits provided by the company. Benefits include (1) insurance—health, life, disability, and liability, (2) paid holiday, vacation, and personal-day policies, (3) retirement, profit sharing, or stock options, and (4) any extras not covered elsewhere, such as day care, fitness counseling, on-the-job training, or tuition reimbursement.

5. **Capital purchase schedule.** Capital purchases are those items the company buys that have a useful life of longer than one year. In most cases, the Internal Revenue Service requires that capital purchases be "depreciated," meaning deducted from taxable revenue over the useful life of the item (several years) rather than all at once. Examples include vehicles, equipment (such as instruments, stage rigs, recording gear, or computers), and real estate.

Besides the tax obligations and benefits, capital purchases usually require that you have an idea in advance of where you're going to get the money to pay for each item. Can you pay from cash on hand or will you need to finance the item? Once again, doing the planning up front helps you anticipate financial needs and prepare accordingly.

Note: Each of the key elements of an operating plan can potentially be the subject of its own book. We've provided an overview here to show how the pieces fit together. We'll expand on the marketing plan element in Section Three. Also see the Reference Section for samples of other elements.

PLAN ELEMENT 5: THE DAILY ACTION LIST

Once you've got an operating plan for the current year, you are ready to go to work. While you don't necessarily have to consult your operating plan every day, you are likely to do so more frequently once you have perspective on the activity flow as presented here.

RELATING BUSINESS PLANNING THEORY TO YOUR MUSIC BUSINESS

Most businesses—music or otherwise—already have parts of the plan but not the whole thing. Little is written down ("It's all up here..."). In many cases, the planning flow goes like this:

Element 1: Product plan

Element 2: Budget (rough revenue plan and estimate of expenses)

Element 3: Daily action list

While this is better than nothing, it leaves a lot to chance.

You may be thinking, "But I'm already in business! This whole thing sounds overly complicated and unrealistic." Or, "I just want to make a decent living in music, not necessarily own a business."

Remember that we are still presenting the perfect-world scenario, offered here as a reference set of tools and definitions. If you are already in business, I encourage you to keep going and take time to fill in the missing plan elements. If you are not yet in business, you are getting a head start by understanding the fundamentals. Chapter Seventeen deals with practical ways to integrate these concepts into your particular situation.

HOW OFTEN DOES THE PLAN CHANGE?

We've already mentioned that the mission and brand positioning statements are designed to last indefinitely. What about the other plan elements? Here are guidelines for revising your business plan.

- Product plan. Revise the product plan once every year and include details that paint a picture of your business two to five years in the future. That way you are always looking several years ahead, with the added benefit of learning from the year that just passed. Your strategic vision may extend many more years into the future, but three years is generally enough for a committed product plan.

- Operating plan. The operating plan is distinctly more short-term in focus. Plan your revenue and expense budgets twelve months in advance by month, then another 12 months by quarter (three-month increments). Add the third year as a 12-month summary, not broken down by month or quarter. As with the product plan, this should be revised each year, adding a year each time so you are always looking three years ahead.

KEY POINTS IN THIS CHAPTER

1. Your strategic business plan helps guide daily action and is key to preserving your integrity, sanity, and cash flow.

2. The planning flow starts with your mission, vision, and values. The other planning flow elements include the brand positioning statement, product plan, and operating plan.

3. Whether you are already in business or just starting, be sure that you have articulated these items so that everything you do is consistent with your long-term goals.

4. The brand positioning statement answers four key questions:
   a. What business are we in?
   b. Who are our customers?
   c. What makes us special?
   d. What's in it for everybody?

5. Understanding what business you are in and who your customers are allows you to pass the "elevator test" with flying colors. Beware of telling people that what you do is "a long story" or that you "wear many hats."

6. Your product plan maps out what you plan to sell over the next three years. Products are the results of your labor and what your customers buy, from services like live performances or bookings to goods like records or other merchandise.

7. The operating plan includes a detailed revenue forecast, marketing plan, budgets and pro forma financial schedules, organization plan, and capital purchase schedule. How to complete each of these is potentially the subject of another book.

8. Practical reality: Things don't always go according to the plan or "by the book" or according to the perfect-world scenario. That is why it is important to revise your plan yearly and monitor your progress monthly.

9. The tactical marketing plan is so important that we will cover it in detail in Section Three ("Building Your Brand").

BUILDING
YOUR BRAND

CHAPTER EIGHT

MARKETING AND SALES ARE THE KEYS TO YOUR SUCCESS

Here we will explore the difference between marketing and sales and how the two work together in the music business. In addition, we'll briefly define the seven elements of any marketing plan—the links in the marketing chain. This will set the stage for Chapters Nine through Fifteen, in which we'll examine each of those links in more detail.

Let's start by looking at music industry statistics again. As of 2001, there are over one million people active in the music industry in North America. Here are related numbers to help put this in perspective:

- There are an estimated 600,000 performing musicians. Of those, over 110,000 are members of the American Federation of Musicians, the union representing musicians in the United States and Canada.

- Music website MP3.com includes 1.5 million registered songs from over 150,000 artists (solo performers and bands).

- There are an estimated 300,000 songwriters who have written millions of songs that are registered with BMI, ASCAP, and SESAC.

- There are hundreds—perhaps thousands—of record labels releasing over 35,000 records per year. In addition, there are countless artists who self-produce records and sell them direct to the public, under the radar of the music industry. The number of new releases has increased dramatically in the past ten years.

- SoundScan tracked the sales of over *280,000* different records in the year 2000. Those released in the past 18 months are considered current, over 18 months are considered *catalog*, and those released over three years ago are considered *deep catalog*.

- Also according to SoundScan, in 2000, less than 1% of new releases accounted for over 50% of all record sales. This means that frightfully few records sell enough to pay back their recording and marketing expenses, let alone provide income for the artists and songwriters involved.

Other numbers are more difficult to determine because so much of what happens in the music industry is not tracked or reported formally. What about:

- All those wedding and private party gigs?

- Show dates booked directly by the artist, with no agent or manager involved?

- Songs that are written and performed but never published?

- Concerts and festivals put on by private and civic groups who do not consider themselves professional promoters?

The music industry is vast, fragmented, and only partially organized. This has its advantages and disadvantages.

COMPETING FOR ATTENTION

The biggest business challenge facing any music person or music business is competing for attention at all levels. There are so many competitors in all categories that the customer's challenge of simply wading through the possible choices can be overwhelming. Consider the following questions:

- How do performers choose what material to perform and record?

- How do agents choose which artists to represent? Which venues are viable for the artists they represent?

- How do record labels or producers decide which artists to sign and produce?

    And of course, the ultimate challenge:

- How do music fans decide which shows to attend and records to buy?

Your marketing plan represents the single most important tool for addressing these issues. It prompts you to not only ask these questions, but determine answers that guide the operation of your music business. Further, when you understand what you're up against—and you've done the homework—you have a huge competitive advantage.

Remember the earlier comment about how so few music businesses have solid business plans? The need for "attention management" (keeping your customers focused on you and your product) intensifies the need for planning, especially as the market becomes even more cluttered with the kind of choices mentioned above.

WHAT IS MARKETING, AND HOW IS IT DIFFERENT FROM SALES?

Let's make a distinction right up front. Marketing and sales are different but intimately related functions in any music business.

Even the dictionary has a hard time differentiating between marketing and sales. The definitions are cross-referenced to the extent that a casual reader could conclude that they mean essentially the same thing. However, they are as different as art and science, yet willing partners in the world of business. Here is a composite dictionary definition:

Marketing: the act of developing products (goods or services) and exposing them for sale to a specified customer base

Sales: the act of causing and expediting a purchase at a specified price, or within a price range

The key word is "specified." It implies that the activities are deliberate as opposed to accidental or random. In less formal language, here are several ways to say the same thing:

- Marketing opens the door. Sales closes it.

- Marketing prepares a sales environment. Sales operates within that environment.

- Marketing defines the product and prepares targeted customers to buy. Sales finishes the job by completing the transfer of goods or services.

- Marketing is the art of communicating with potential customers. Sales is the science of converting potential customers into real paying customers.

- Marketing hooks 'em. Sales reels 'em in.

THE FOUR FUNCTIONS OF MARKETING

Let's turn the definitions into examples of functional activities in each of the two areas, starting with marketing. When I've asked clients and seminar audiences, "What comes to mind when I say the word marketing?," the most frequent answer is "advertising." While advertising and related promotional activities are indeed part of marketing, they are only one small aspect among many others.

Here are examples of marketing functions, organized in four key areas:

Marketing Function 1. Planning and Positioning the Product

- Develop product definitions and product strategy

- Monitor business conditions and competitive activity; conduct market research

- Perform market tests, such as dress rehearsals, focus groups, and regional record rollouts

- Model comprehensive marketing plans

- Forecast and control inventory, ranging from tour schedules to CDs in stock

Marketing Function 2. Communicating with Your Target Market

- Tell your company story; build your image through publicity and related efforts

- Provide newsletters, press releases, website content, and other communications to your target customers and the general public

- Handle press relations, including editorial placement of reviews, interviews, and articles

- Maintain industry relations; participate in professional organizations; attend conferences, trade shows, and other music business events

Marketing Function 3. Managing Customer Relationships

- Advise and assist customers on a continual basis

- Qualify customer requests and refer them to the proper follow-up person

- Handle charity or sponsorship requests; participate in benefit concerts; make donations to nonprofit organizations

- Follow-up on complaints and suggestions

Marketing Function 4. Advertising and Promotion

- Plan, produce, and schedule advertising with the media

- Plan and produce promotion materials, including photos, biographies, press kits, and merchandising materials

- Plan and coordinate trade shows, showcases, conferences, and special events

- Plan and locate sources for premiums, incentives, and identity items, such as T-shirts, jackets, fly swatters, refrigerator magnets, key rings, and the like

- Fulfill and track prospective customer inquiries

Once again, notice that while advertising and promotion are important, they are among many other marketing functions.

THE FOUR FUNCTIONS OF SALES

Let's take a look at sales functions in a similar fashion. Many people think of sales only in terms of negotiating and processing contract paperwork or orders for records and merchandise. There's more to sales than just asking for the order.

Here are examples of sales functions, organized in four key areas:

Sales Function 1. Achieving Sales Objectives, or "Hitting the Numbers"

- Negotiate and develop relationships with target customers

- Train and support sales representatives, such as agents, or dealer salespersons, such as distributor or record store personnel

- Secure and expedite sales orders, including all contract paperwork

- Track sales and expense results; monitor sales revenue vs. quota, and expenses vs. budget

Sales Function 2. Participating in Events

- Get involved in promotions or special sales activities like artist showcases, clinics, or in-store events with record merchants

- Lead or participate in sales meetings, key client negotiations, and sales presentations

- Attend trade shows, conferences, and seminars

Sales Function 3. Managing the Sales Territory

- Plan and develop product distribution or client relations within an assigned territory

- Control use of free product samples, including unpaid auditions, promotion-only records, or complimentary show tickets

- Develop relationships with key customers' and influencers' staff, such as event promoters' crew members or booking agency assistants, who do not necessarily buy but can influence a purchase.

- Implement sales and marketing programs in the field, like promoting a song or record at a retail store or radio station

- Balance office and field travel—sell face-to-face as well as on the phone and via e-mail

- Monitor business conditions and the competitive environment; report details to the company regularly

Sales Function 4. Handling General Administrative Tasks

- Maintain equipment and supplies as required—from office phones to personal digital assistants, from paper clips to promotion materials

- Interface with internal departments such as sales, marketing, and accounting, and contract service providers such as agents, business managers, recording studios, or tour crew

- Do the paperwork, including expense reports, sales forecasts, travel itineraries, special correspondence, and maintenance of contact databases

Note: *Contract* paperwork and collection of payment comes under key sales function number 1: Achieving Sales Objectives. Why? Because (and here is one of the greatest pieces of business wisdom I've learned) "a sale is not a sale until it is paid."

THE SEVEN LINKS IN THE MARKETING CHAIN

Textbook marketing (a term referring to the basic fundamentals of marketing taught in most business schools) talks about the "four p's" of your marketing plan: product, pricing, promotion, and place. In our consulting practice, we expand these four elements to seven, and call them the links in the marketing chain. Here are brief descriptions of the seven links:

Link 1: Product strategy. Identify the goods and services you currently offer and plan to offer over time.

Link 2: Pricing strategy. Understand how much things sell for or *what the market will bear.*

Link 3: Promotional strategy. Create media advertising (print and broadcast), publicity, sales literature, websites, trade shows, showcase performances, and direct marketing materials.

Link 4: Sales channel strategy and place of business. A sales channel is an intermediary who purchases your product for resale. A place of business has two dimensions: geographical territory and your personal workspace—whether a home office or a corporate facility. For performers and promoters, place of business also includes target performance venues.

Link 5: Salesforce strategy. Decide who does the selling, what skills your salespeople need, and how much it costs to employ good ones.

Link 6: End-user or audience and buyer profiles. Identify key characteristics of target customers and understand their buying habits and preferences.

Link 7: Competitive environment. Identify your competitors' strengths and weaknesses, and anticipate their activities over time.

Note: Each of the above links is covered in detail in Chapters Nine through Fifteen.

Now you can easily see that marketing is much more than advertising and promotion. As the old saying goes: "The chain is only as strong as the weakest link."

For example, you could have the greatest act in the world (link 1), but if you do not understand your audience (link 6) and competitors (link 7), you may accidentally price (link 2) or promote (link 3) your act the wrong way or use the wrong salespeople (link 5) or sell through the wrong channels (link 4).

All combinations work the same way. You could have a great agent and beautiful promotional materials, but if the act (the product) is weak or the audience is too fragmented to target, the results are compromised. The chain is only as strong as the weakest link.

At this point, it may sound more complicated than it actually is—don't worry. We're about to explore how to develop your product strategy, and examine each of the seven links in detail.

KEY POINTS IN THIS CHAPTER

1. There's lots of competition out there. Your music business is one among tens of thousands vying for attention and market share.

2. Lots of competition indicates lots of market opportunities. This is good. The sheer number of music businesses means that your buyers have many positive product choices.

3. Your biggest challenge is competing for the buyer's attention. This points to the absolute necessity of a marketing plan and strong marketing and sales functions.

4. Marketing and sales are different from each other, but intimately related. Marketing hooks 'em. Sales reels 'em in.

5. The four marketing functions are: (1) planning and positioning the product, (2) communicating with your target market, (3) managing customer relationships, and (4) advertising and promotion.

6. The four sales functions are: (1) achieving sales objectives, or "hitting the numbers," (2) participating in events, (3) managing sales territory, and (4) handling general administrative tasks.

7. Any marketing plan has seven links in the marketing chain. The seven links are: (1) product strategy, (2) pricing strategy, (3) promotional strategy, (4) sales channel strategy and place of business, (5) salesforce strategy, (6) end-user or audience and buyer profiles, and (7) competitive environment.

8. As the old saying goes, "The chain is only as strong as the weakest link." If one of the seven links is weak or missing, your business potential and results are compromised.

CHAPTER NINE

DEVELOPING YOUR PRODUCT STRATEGY

L et's examine the first link in your marketing chain—product strategy. At the strategic level, you decide what product category or categories you will offer over time. At the tactical level, it's time to get specific and go into much more detail.

MUSIC INDUSTRY PRODUCTS: EXAMPLES OF GOODS AND SERVICES

Let's look at the music goods and services matrix one more time:

Your Industry Role	Product Example	Goods	Services
Performing musician	Live performances		x
Booking agent	Secure bookings		x
Manager	Provide management services		x
Record label	Recorded music (CDs, etc.)	x	
Event promoter	Entertainment experiences		x
Songwriter	Original compositions		x
Music teacher	Learning experiences		x
Merchandiser	T-shirts, jackets, identity items	x	
Publisher	Songbooks and sheet music; song promotion and royalty administration	x	x

Now let's go a little deeper. Here are examples of music business products that are likely to be familiar to most readers:

1. Live performances—concerts, festivals, club dates, and private events such as weddings, parties, corporate meetings, etc. If you are a performer, an agent, a manager, or a promoter, you are involved in live performances as a product category.

2. Record sales—any delivery medium for music: audio, video, or multimedia via compact disc, tape, vinyl, DVD, VHS, or digital download. Records are sold through distribution (retailers, mail order, or websites) or direct from the artist. Virtually all music people get involved with record sales on some level.

3. Music publishing—royalties from broadcast airplay (radio, television, films, Internet) and record sales. While songwriters, publishers, and recording artists are most involved with publishing, agents and managers also play a role in many cases. Songs are also published in sheet music or songbook form. This gives the songwriters and performers another product opportunity.

4. Business services—booking, management, accounting, publicity, promotion, and tour management. Primarily the domain of agents and managers, lawyers, accountants, and other specialists who also provide business services as products.

5. Technical services—recording, mastering, graphic design, web content production, sound reinforcement, instrument repair, and even tour bus maintenance. (While somewhat outside the scope of this book, be aware that technical services are "products" and essential elements of the product plans of those service providers.)

JACK OF ALL TRADES, MASTER OF SOME . . .

At most levels of the music industry, individuals and firms offer a variety of music business products, crossing over within the basic product categories. Here are some examples. Can you relate to any of them?

- Performing songwriters sell live performances, songs to other artists, songbooks, and records.

- Nonperforming songwriters sell songs, songbooks, and records. Many establish their own publishing or record production companies.

- Booking agents sell consulting services to promoters, and management services to artists, in addition to securing performance bookings for artists.

- Managers provide advice and business service to artists and may also operate record labels, performance venues, or publishing companies.

- Promoters may operate record labels, management firms, or publishing companies in addition to presenting concerts and festivals to the general public.

- Many performers do it all: write and record the songs, book and perform show dates, and operate record labels, booking agencies, and publishing companies. While no one has hard statistics, it is likely that self-managed performing songwriters represent the largest single category of music people.

YOUR PRODUCT MIX CHANGES OVER TIME

Few music businesses start by doing everything at once. Consider our original band story from the overview that opened this book (page 5). The group started as performers, then booked themselves, and later recorded and sold records. Songwriters get into publishing and record-label work. Agencies start promotion and business services divisions.

The reverse is also common. Multi-category businesses may occasionally delete products or spin them off into separate companies.

Though you don't have to do everything yourself, or everything at once. This is a key business planning principle and one which music people often overlook. Further, it is valuable to plan your product strategy several years into the future. Try this brief exercise. Fill in the chart below by checking the boxes that are relevant. (Note: This planning matrix is also in the Reference Section and on the CD-ROM.)

Product Category	This Year	Next Year	Year Two	Year Three
Live performances	_____	_____	_____	_____
Secure bookings	_____	_____	_____	_____
Provide management services	_____	_____	_____	_____
Recorded music (CDs, etc.)	_____	_____	_____	_____
Entertainment experiences—tickets	_____	_____	_____	_____
Original compositions	_____	_____	_____	_____
T-shirts, jackets, identity items	_____	_____	_____	_____
Song promotion and royalty administration	_____	_____	_____	_____
Other (specify):	_____	_____	_____	_____

UNDERSTANDING PRODUCT LIFE CYCLES—THE SIX PHASES

Each product has a "life cycle" roughly analogous to that of human life: conception, birth, childhood, adolescence, adulthood, maturity, seniority, and death. The business world uses slightly different terms and organizes the product life cycle into six phases.

- **Phase 0:** Research and development. This phase occurs *before* the product is ready to sell. For all music people, this is when you do market research, analysis, and planning. As a performer or songwriter, it is when you are rehearsing an act, writing original material, or recording. If you are an agent or manager, it's when you are assembling a roster of artists to represent and developing the business services you will offer them. As a promoter, the research and development phase is when you cultivate relationships with artists, agents, and venue owners.

Note: Research and development is called phase 0 (as opposed to phase 1) because business schools and textbooks refer to the first phase as an *introduction* and presume that the development work has been done before the product is launched. Thus you have six phases, though it looks like five.

- **Phase 1:** Introduction. As a performer, this phase represents your first gigs, which are often performed for little or no money and to small audiences. As a songwriter, the introductory phase may focus on self-produced demo records or covers of your compositions by artists that you know personally. As an agent, it may mean that your agency focuses on local clubs, colleges, and private events. The same holds true for promoters, who often begin with small venues and low-budget productions.

- **Phase 2:** Early growth. In this phase, the business starts to take off. As your business gains more customers and revenue, the audience profile changes. Performers advance to higher paying and more prestigious gigs. Songwriters begin to place material with established artists. Airplay creeps into the picture for recording acts. Agents and managers take on additional acts to represent and may branch out geographically. Promoters use multiple venues (small and large) and present shows more frequently.

- **Phase 3:** Late growth or shake-out. In music industry terms, this phase is when acts *break nationally*. It is also the phase that most music people and businesses aspire to. Artists perform consistently in larger venues, command higher fees, and tour over wider geographic areas. Songwriters earn increasing royalties from record sales, broadcast airplay, and print music sales (sheet music and songbooks). Agents and managers prune their rosters to focus on established artists. Promoters continue to present shows more frequently and to larger audiences—sometimes in venues that they own or control exclusively.

Note: The term *shake-out* refers to the fact that many businesses merge, sell to another company, or go out of business during this phase. There are fewer competitors in the market in phase 3 (and subsequent phases) than in phases 1 and 2.

- **Phase 4:** Maturity or saturation. After a while, an artist's record sales, airplay, and concert attendance reach a plateau—they stop growing. While the numbers may be large, the audiences and the performance fees are not getting bigger. The market is saturated. Fans have had enough, and newer artists (particularly those in phase 2 and 3 of their careers) have captured the imagination of the audience. This has a ripple effect on agents, managers, and promoters. There is plenty of business to do, but less buzz than in the late-growth phase.

- **Phase 5:** Decline. This is the phase that everyone wants to avoid, as it signifies a loss of popularity, marketability, and earning power. This is when former "name" artists perform on package shows or festivals, cruise ships, and corporate events. While the fee per performance may be enough to make a living, the average fee and number of dates are less than in earlier phases. Records may become cutouts or *mid-line* releases. Acts may tour on the strength of a greatest-hits release versus a record with all-new material. As in the saturation phase, performers' ability to draw an audience and sell records has a direct impact on agents, managers, songwriters, and promoters. They are usually already looking elsewhere for new artists—fresh blood at earlier career stages, or earlier phases in the product life cycle.

All products go through the life cycle from conception to birth, childhood, adolescence, adulthood, maturity, seniority, and death. The business world refers to six phases as shown above: research and development, introduction, early growth, late growth or shake-out, maturity or saturation, and decline.

On first glance, it is easy to conclude that decline and death are inevitable. You may ask yourself, "If that's the case, then why bother?" Or, "How do I get to phase 3—late growth—and simply stay there?" That's actually the better of the two questions and one that many music people simply never address. Some music business careers begin and end within one year. Others last for decades.

You've heard the expression, "one-hit wonder," which refers to performers or songwriters who achieve a measure of recognition (and maybe even get rich) based on a single song. I've only met a few music people who aspired to be one-hit wonders.

Then there's the other end of the spectrum. Consider the work of classic artists past and present who have performed for over fifty years: Duke Ellington, Louis Armstrong, Bill Monroe, Frankie Yankovic, Les Paul, B.B. King, Tony Bennett, Pete Seeger, Ella Fitzgerald, Etta James, Isaac Stern. Lots of people admire these artists and others like them. Outside of having the requisite talent, planning and business skills make the largest difference between the two extremes.

HOW LONG DOES EACH PHASE LAST?

Can you accurately predict how long your product will take to develop, launch, and mature? The short answers are "it varies" and "no." That means that there are no firm rules and certainly no guarantees. That said, you can model each phase as part of your planning process. That's what business planning is all about—getting control of your business.

The goal is to get through research and development and launch your product relatively quickly. Let's say that takes months as opposed to years. Then the challenge is to build your business through the introduction and early-growth phases and get to the late-growth phase as quickly as possible. While that may take a few years as opposed to months, you can still make a living and enjoy your music business along the way.

Think of examples from music genres that are familiar to you. Do you know any performers, songwriters, agents, managers, or promoters who fall into each of the phase categories? Where are *you* currently? The relevant point here is to relate your current product life cycle phase to your product strategy for the next two years, and then be sure that the rest of your marketing plan (pricing strategy, promotional platform, distribution channel, sales program) is consistent with that strategy. We'll come back to this in the rest of Section Three as we examine the other links in the marketing chain.

KEY POINTS IN THIS CHAPTER

1. *Products* include goods and services. The first step in developing a product strategy is to understand your current products and product mix.

2. Products are what you get paid for. Performers get paid for live performances and recording; songwriters and composers for creating original material; agents and managers for securing bookings and providing business services; promoters for presenting events and providing entertainment experiences for target audiences.

3. Don't try to be a musical "jack of all trades." While many artists start out multitasking (booking and recording while writing and performing), it is difficult to master all aspects of the music business.

4. Your product mix is likely to change over time. Start by assessing what you are doing now, then look ahead three years and see what products you will add or delete. This is an example of strategic planning—deciding now where you want to be in the future.

5. All products go through a life cycle from conception to birth, childhood, adolescence, adulthood, maturity, seniority, and death. This is called the product life cycle.

6. The business world organizes the product life cycle into six phases (0) research and development, (1) introduction, (2) early growth, (3) late growth or shake-out, (4) maturity or saturation, and (5) decline.

7. Every product goes through the six phases consecutively, each taking a different amount of time. Your mission is to get through the introduction and early-growth phases as quickly as possible. The volume and long-term profit potential are in the late-growth and maturity phases.

8. Successful music people make the late-growth phase last as long as possible. It's the phase associated with the largest audiences, financial rewards, and "buzz."

9. Each phase represents a different customer profile and requires a different marketing plan: product configuration, pricing strategy, promotional platform, distribution channel, and sales program.

CHAPTER TEN

YOUR PRICING STRATEGY

The second link in the marketing chain is your pricing strategy. For some music people, setting prices can be mysterious, sensitive, and a bit scary. Pricing strategy involves the decisions you make about pricing before you go to market. How do you set prices? Do they change over time? How do you know if your prices are market worthy? This chapter explores these issues and provides guidelines for preventing mistakes and optimizing revenue opportunities.

AN AGENT'S TALE

There's an old story that booking agents tell. It is meant to both amuse and inform.

An agent was interviewing an artist to see if they could develop a business relationship.

Agent: "How much do you charge for a show date?"

Artist: "$150,000 a performance."

Agent: "At that price, you won't get many dates."

Artist: "At that price, I don't *need* many dates!"

It's a fact of business that few artists are paid $150,000 per date on a regular basis. The amusing part (at least to experienced agents) is that some naive artists think they can just name their price. The practical lesson is that artists can set pricing *goals* and work toward ever-increasing per-performance fees, based on pricing *objectives*. This ties to the product life cycle concept. Let's turn this into a set of practical guidelines.

CHARGING WHAT THE MARKET WILL BEAR— THREE FACTORS

You probably have heard the expression, "Charge what the market will bear." This implies (correctly) that the market (*customers* or *clients*) determines pricing in the long run. Three key factors influence how much customers are willing to pay.

Pricing Factor 1: Supply and Demand

This is a fundamental business principle. Prices go up or down based on the balance between *supply*, or product availability, and *demand*, or number of potential customers in the market.

For example, a music store may mark down the prices of instruments or gear in stock if they have too much inventory or if customers are not asking for the product. Conversely, the same store may sell custom guitars at list price because the maker's output is limited and the market is small but willing to pay a higher asking price for a unique instrument.

This principle applies to some, but not all, categories of music people and their products. Below are two contrasting examples:

- Barbra Streisand, Madonna, or the Rolling Stones (among other big-name acts) command large performance fees because they perform relatively rarely and fans are willing to pay higher than average ticket prices to see them (more demand than supply).

- On the other hand, many performers are often locked into the talent budget of a club or festival and take what the venue or promoter offers. If the act doesn't like the price, the promoter hires someone else (more supply than demand).

Pricing Factor 2: Pricing Conventions and Traditions

Here's a common expression: "We've always done it that way." Every industry, including music, has its time-tested pricing guidelines or methods. Here are some music industry examples:

- Sidemen and technicians are paid flat rates per performance, tour, or season. The amount is negotiated in advance and stays the same over the contract period.

- Booking agents charge a flat percentage of performance revenue, usually in the 10–20% range.

- Managers also charge a flat percentage, often based on artists' total revenue (performances, royalties, recording advances, etc.), usually in the 10–25% range. When compensated on the high end of the percentage range, the manager may pay outside booking agent commissions from the manager's share.

- Recording artists and songwriters earn royalties at rates that are established by law and administered by the music publishing industry. While the rates change occasionally, the individual artist has little or no control over them.

- The record industry has its own set of pricing conventions. For example, most single-disc CDs with 40 to 70 minutes of music sell for approximately $10 wholesale and $12 to $18 retail. Production and marketing costs or the relative popularity of the artist have little effect on the selling price.

- Concert, festival, and club ticket prices vary with the notoriety of the act(s), size of the venue, and price of competitive entertainment offerings (sports events, movies, theme park admissions, etc.). As a result, live music ticket prices paid by fans range from $0 (free) for subsidized events like community festivals to over $100 for premium seats at major concerts and festivals.

Pricing Factor 3: Your Sales and Marketing Ability

Regardless of musical talent, some acts are marketed and sold more effectively than others. This capability is developed over time and is fundamental to the premise of this book. Consider the following examples:

- Acts with professional-looking promotion materials often command higher prices. This is not simply based on the materials, but on the idea that the club or promoter can use the materials (photos, bios, press clippings, etc.) to help charge higher ticket prices and draw a larger crowd.

- Live acts with recorded product can generally charge more than unrecorded acts.

- Recording artists and songwriters with established track records (strong recording and airplay history) can potentially command higher royalty advances than unproven artists.

- Agencies and managers that market their acts consistently over time develop a reputation for representing specific types of acts or catering to a target market segment. This allows them to negotiate more firmly and build artists' pricing as audiences and demand grows.

- Promoters with established track records can help break in new artists and develop different music genres based on their ability to package proven entertainment experiences with new ones. This ties to increasing both ticket prices and audience sizes over time.

THE THREE BASIC PRICING STRATEGIES

Every business has a pricing strategy, whether it is conscious of it or not. In the classic or textbook business sense, there are three basic strategic pricing options: low-cost producer, differentiation, and hybrid. Below we'll look at two examples of each strategy, the first in each from outside the music business.

1. Low-cost producer strategy.

In this approach, the supplier prices to the low end of the market and earns acceptable profits by controlling internal costs. Our examples:

- Generic or "store brands" at the grocery store. Ever wonder how your local supermarket can afford to charge so much less for its own can of soup compared to the nationally advertised brands? In some cases, the ingredients and quality are essentially the same, but the store brand is cheaper than the name brand. This is because they have learned how to control costs, charge less, and still make an acceptable profit margin. Pricing below the competition is a conscious marketing decision.

- Independent vs. major label recording projects. As stated above, records sell for about the same price no matter what label they are on or who the artist is. How can independent record labels afford to compete with the mass-marketed majors? In many cases, the independent label controls recording, production, and marketing costs differently from the major label. This allows the label and artist to make an acceptable margin at lower unit volumes.

Note: Simply watching expenses and looking for ways to undercut competitive prices do not constitute a low-cost producer strategy. Any well-run music business pays attention to its production and operating costs. Those adopting this pricing strategy deliberately find ways to turn cost control into higher profits.

2. Differentiation strategy.

Here the supplier charges as high a price as possible, based on the product's features and competitive advantages. Differentiation assumes that there are aspects of each competitor's product that can be distinguished easily. Those features and benefits are promoted to those customers who are willing to pay a higher price for something different (and presumably better). Again, two examples:

- Designer clothes vs. department store brands. This is the converse of the grocery-store example above, and one that most people can relate to. Whether you shop at Wal-Mart, Saks Fifth Avenue, or a designer boutique, you can choose among brands of blue jeans with slightly different styling and features—and radically different prices. The designer-label clothes have a feature/advantage/benefit story to tell, and sell for more.

- Established acts vs. new or unproven acts. It's common in the music world for established acts to draw crowds that are larger and/or willing to pay higher ticket prices. If the music essentially sounds the same, what difference does it make? Entertainment is entertainment, right? From the fan's point of view, the answer is: "Not necessarily." The established act is more likely to have that "story" to tell: recordings, good reviews, fan buzz, or legacy. More on this in later chapters.

Most music businesses are based on the differentiation pricing strategy. The goal is to increase prices over time based on the marketable difference between you and your competitors. While the market will bear only so much (in terms of performance fees, ticket prices, etc.), the range is wide.

3. Hybrid strategy.

In this approach, the supplier offers more than one product and uses both the low-cost producer and differentiation strategies selectively. Some products may be viewed as *commodities* and are subject to competitive market pressures. Others can be *differentiated* and priced accordingly. The examples:

- In-stock vs. special-order motor vehicles. When you shop for a car, you have a choice of buying one "off the lot" or having one made to order. The dealer prices the cars on the lot to be competitive with the market and conducive to quick sales. If you want something special—like the upgraded sound system or custom-color upholstery—you pay more and wait longer. The fact that the dealer offers both is an example of a hybrid pricing strategy.

- Multiple music products. As described in Chapter Nine, many music people offer more than one category of product. For example, a performer is likely to price live shows using a differentiation strategy, but to price self-produced records using a low-cost producer strategy. Likewise, an agent or manager may represent established acts who can name their own price in addition to newer acts that conform to promoters' budgets or opening-act policies.

While product differentiation drives the music industry, many music businesses end up with a hybrid pricing strategy due to their mix of products. Further, those who are reliant on income derived by charging a percentage of some other revenue (songwriter royalties, agent and manager commissions), need to be conscious of both cost control and techniques to increase fees on a per-transaction basis.

CHANGING PRICES AND REVENUE PLANNING

A key part of your long-term pricing strategy is to forecast your revenue several years in advance. When you look at your sales plan over a longer period of time, you can apply the fundamentals described in this chapter to your best advantage. We'll cover goals and objectives in detail in Chapter Sixteen. In the meantime, here is a simple formula to start the process of planning revenue.

Revenue = units sold x average selling price

Sounds simple, and it is. This formula applies to all music people, regardless of what you do. Worksheets in the Reference Section apply to the various specialties: performers, songwriters, agents, managers, and promoters. For now, let's use the example of a performing act.

	This Year	Next Year	Year Two	Year Three
Show dates per year	30	60	90	120
Average $ per date	$200	$500	$1,000	$2,000
Total performance $	**$6,000**	**$30,000**	**$90,000**	**$240,000**

Remember that this is a simplified example, just to show the fundamentals of revenue planning. When you do this with your own numbers, you will find that it is often a wake-up call that you aren't charging enough. How do I know that? Because I've done it myself, and I know music people who have done it and ended up changing their pricing strategies as a result.

See how the table on page 79 corresponds to the product planning matrix in Chapter Nine? This is a recurring theme. When your three-year objectives are staring you in the face, it is much easier to make operational business decisions than if you had written nothing down or had only thought a few months ahead.

WHAT TYPICALLY HAPPENS IN THE MUSIC INDUSTRY

Let's go back to the "$150,000 a date" story (page 75). The artist was naming the price and the agent knew it was unrealistic. Here are examples of the consequences of *not* having a realistic pricing strategy:

- Never enough revenue to make a living. Too many music people think that price increases either never come or will simply be offered by generous customers. There's another old ironic expression, which goes like this: "I plan to lose $100 on every date, but make it up on volume." Yikes! It doesn't work that way. If you are losing money on every date, figure out how to either increase fees, lower costs, or both.

- Pricing out of the market. While it's true that "at $150,000 a date I don't need to work much," it is possible that if your prices are too high, you simply will not get any work.

- Costs get out of control. As discussed in the three pricing strategies above, it is essential to understand your expenses before you determine selling prices.

- Inaccurate or limiting image or reputation. Ask yourself how you would like to be regarded relative to pricing. While there is no right or wrong answer, see which of the following pricing images best suits you.

"Always plays for the door (or tips)."

"Cheap—I don't know how they stay in business."

"Penny-wise and pound-foolish."

"Willing to work for anything."

"A great value—we all make money."

"Premium quality, premium price."

"Overpriced—you're paying for the name."

People in creative fields like music frequently adopt a differentiation pricing strategy, either consciously or unconsciously. Specifically, many music people believe that their product is unique and price it as high as possible. This can apply to show dates, tickets, and recording and publishing advances, as well as business or technical services.

Those with business plans and market awareness will best understand the differentiation approach and work toward it long-term. That's part of an overall plan to make more money, have more fun, and stay in business longer. Even a booking agent paid on a fixed commission schedule works to drive acts' prices higher whenever possible.

Others look out in the market and set prices at or below what competitors are charging. While this can be a viable approach, I believe that many music people leave money on the table, unconsciously assuming that they have no influence on customers' budgets or willingness to pay.

Not enough music people actually have a conscious pricing strategy. As a result, they default to charging too much or too little. Sometimes this works, but it frequently leads to problems.

Some artists charge too little and end up subsidizing the music by working the proverbial day job. Others burn out prematurely due to overwork at under market prices. Others charge too much too soon, and can't get enough work to stay in business.

HOW TO AVOID PRICING PROBLEMS AND OPTIMIZE REVENUE

Pricing problems lead to revenue problems. Music people seldom have enough money. Hmmm, there might be a connection here! While you may not be able to name your price, there are three things you can do to avoid problems.

Pricing Tactic 1. Understand the range of prices charged by others who do what you do before you establish or quote prices in the marketplace.

Pricing Tactic 2. Do your revenue planning using the three-year view and formula before making major business decisions such as going on tour, cutting the next record, hiring additional people, or investing in promotional materials.

Pricing Tactic 3: Understand that you have a higher degree of control over how things change over time than you might first imagine. This ties to the importance of doing things consciously versus unconsciously.

KEY POINTS IN THIS CHAPTER

1. Pricing strategy involves conscious decisions on how you set prices over time.

2. Many music people think they have to work for whatever is offered, or that they can name their own price. Both of these extremes are unrealistic. Understand the range of prices applicable to your type of product before constructing your own pricing strategy.

3. The market influences pricing as it relates to *supply and demand*. If there is more supply than demand (such as opening acts looking for exposure), the average market price is relatively low. If there is more demand than supply (like the one and only Rolling Stones) the market price is relatively high.

4. The market sets the price, but only to a point. There are music industry traditions and conventions to work around, especially involving agent/manager commissions, publishing and performance royalties, and record sales.

5. You can control and manage your pricing over time, if it is realistic. Work toward increasing prices and revenue as you develop your business.

6. From a classic business standpoint, there are three basic pricing strategies relevant to the music industry: low-cost producer, differentiation, and hybrid. Most music businesses strive for higher earnings through increased fees over time, pointing to a long-term differentiation strategy.

7. Revenue = units sold x average selling price. You need a pricing strategy to forecast revenue and create budgets that look ahead three years in concert with your product strategy.

8. Many music people charge too little as opposed to too much. Using a conscious planning approach, you can often avoid not making enough money, allowing costs to get out of control, or developing the wrong image.

9. Pricing problems can be prevented in many cases with a well-planned, long-term pricing strategy. You have a higher degree of control over how things change over time than you might imagine.

CHAPTER ELEVEN

PROMOTION, BRANDING, AND ADVERTISING

Now we turn to the third link in the marketing chain, promotional strategy, which has three distinct elements: promotion, branding, and advertising. It is vitally important to remember that these three elements are just *one link in the chain*. They do *not* constitute the whole of marketing, as is often thought. That said, let's examine your promotional strategy.

As with marketing and sales, the dictionary cross-references advertising and promotion to the extent that a casual reader would conclude that they are the same thing. For our purposes here, let's use the following definition:

Promotion is the process of delivering *controlled* messages about you and your products to your target customers, audience, and other stakeholders. Stakeholders may include your staff, vendors, community, financial investors or creditors, or the general public.

A WORD ABOUT BRANDING

Just like marketing, advertising, and promotion, we hear the word "branding" used in a variety of business contexts. So what is branding, anyway?

Branding is the creation of indelible images of you and your products in the minds of your target customers, audience, and stakeholders. Examples of music business brands include your name or stage name, your company name, names of songs, records, festivals, concert series, clubs, and other venues. Brands can consist of both words and graphic images (logos and trademarks) associated with your business.

Your brand is the symbol of what you do and what you stand for. While music fans are unlikely to say, "I really like the Rolling Stones' big lips brand symbol" in casual conversation, they are likely to recognize that brand when they see it and think of what it stands for: the mark of the "world's greatest rock 'n' roll band."

Likewise with jazz fans. All you have to do is say "Duke" or "Louis" or "Miles" or "Bird" or "Wynton" in a jazz context and an image comes to mind.

Or how about country music? Hank, Willie, Garth, Reba, Loretta . . . the list goes on. We could do the same for virtually every genre of music. The name, logo, and other images remind fans and music business people of something special (hopefully something good) about the artist and their music (read: "products").

These artists sent controlled messages to their target customers, audience, and stakeholders consistently and over a long enough period of time to have become brands. We'll come back to this concept in Section Four ("Applying the Fundamentals in Your Music Business").

THE PROMOTIONAL TOOLBOX—TEN TYPES OF TOOLS

There are many ways to promote. It is beyond the scope of this book to present an exhaustive list of promotional tactics or to suggest how to use them. There are many good books and other educational materials—some geared to the music business—already available on the topic of promotion. For now, we will focus on brief definitions that you can use as a guide as you develop your marketing plan and build your promotional toolbox.

Tool 1: Advertising

Here's an irony in the world of promotion. Ask ten people this question:

"What's the best form of advertising?"

What comes to your mind? Even people who are not marketers are likely to answer, "Word of mouth." This means that the most credible and cost-effective way to get a promotional message into someone's mind is to have it delivered in person by someone with knowledge and authority. Wow! That's easier said than done.

The term "missionary selling" means meeting face-to-face with prospective customers and sharing your sales message one person or one small group at a time. Ever have someone try to sell you magazine subscriptions or Girl Scout cookies, or get you to vote for a political candidate through in-person canvassing?

Door to door or "lead them by the hand" promotion and sales may work for some products, but it is generally impractical for selling concert tickets, records, or music business services. You get the picture.

Advertising is the act of delivering a paid promotional message to a target audience. A key word here is "paid." You pay someone to deliver your message to a predetermined or target audience.

There are two types of advertising: trade and consumer. Trade ads are sometimes called "business to business" or "B2B" ads. Consumer ads focus on end-users or the general public. Advertising media categories include print (magazines and newspapers), broadcast (radio and television), outdoor (billboards and other signage), and online (websites and e-mail).

For example, if you are releasing a record and want to promote it to record retailers, you might advertise in a trade publication like *Billboard* magazine.

If you already have distribution, or sell directly to the public, you might advertise the same record in targeted consumer magazines like *Rolling Stone, Wired, Guitar Player, Utne Reader,* or *The New Yorker.*

Promoters often use local radio and entertainment sections in newspapers as advertising media. Agents and managers may promote their rosters of acts in trade publications or directories. Songwriters seldom use advertising as a promotional tool, but a music publisher may advertise a song or record in a broadcast industry trade magazine like *Gavin* or *Radio and Records.*

So what's the irony in this? It's that while word of mouth *is* the most effective form of advertising, it simply is not efficient by itself to get your message across to the wider audience. That efficiency in reaching many people simultaneously is the rationale behind using advertising as a promotional tool.

Tool 2: Publicity

Media advertising has a place in many marketing campaigns, but there are alternatives. Publicity (also referred to as public relations or "PR") is another form of media, but is clearly not advertising.

Publicity is the act of delivering an unpaid educational message to a target audience. The key words here are "unpaid" and "educational." While you do pay for advertising space or time, you do not pay for publicity.

The media's rationale is that an educational message (as opposed to a "here's the product and price, come and get it" ad message) is of general interest to their target readers, viewers, and listeners. They need news and other material on a constant basis. You make the editor's job easier by providing information on your activities and products.

Note: There are costs associated with generating publicity. It is not "free advertising" as is commonly believed. Further, you may pay for the delivery of your own publicity in the form of newsletters, press releases, press conferences, and press tours or interviews. You cover your own production and travel expenses in the hope that the media will pick up your story.

Here's a "trade" example of the value of publicity. Put yourself in the position of a booking agent or talent buyer, reading trade publications and attending trade shows. If you saw an artist's advertisement in the magazine or show directory, you are likely to skip over it. If you saw an interview, tour itinerary, or record review covering the same artist, you may be more likely to take notice and take some sort of action, like checking out a live show or listening to a record.

Continuing this example, if you read an interview and want to know more about the artist, you may need to consult a directory or some other form of advertising to get complete contact information (address, telephone, e-mail, website). So, as you can see, advertising and publicity work together.

Tool 3: Sales Literature

Sales literature includes brochures and catalogs that describe and depict your product. This is tangible print material, which you can deliver to prospective customers via mail, online, or in person. By the way, the word "promo" is an abbreviation for "promotion." Here are examples:

- Performer: Artists can provide their own business cards, biographies, photos, reprints of reviews, interviews and other publicity, testimonials, posters, fliers, and handbills.

- Songwriter: Non-performers can provide the same items, plus lists of publishing and recording credits.

- Agent or manager: In addition to the materials provided by represented artists, agents and managers often produce materials that focus on their respective companies. These include artist rosters, mission statements, itineraries, sample contracts and riders, and brochures about services for target clients.

- Promoter: Along with the basics like business cards and company brochures, promoters often use posters, handbills, and fliers as tools to promote specific shows.

Tool 4: Demo Recordings and Other Collateral Materials

Collateral materials (also referred to simply as "collateral") include those promotional items that work with, but do not take the place of, basic print sales literature. As with the other tools in your promotional toolbox, your collateral materials are designed to help promote your product to your target customer.

Here are examples of collateral materials:

- Performer and songwriter: demo recordings (audio CDs, video tapes and discs, and CD-ROMs), souvenir items, songbooks, tour or concert programs

- Agent or manager: compilation recordings featuring multiple artists

- Promoter: souvenir programs from prior shows, compilation CDs, testimonial videos of interviews with artists and audience members

Tool 5: Direct Marketing

Direct marketing is a catchall term that includes any promotional activity in which direct contact is made with the target customer. While advertising and publicity are *indirect* promotional methods, direct marketing—also called direct response marketing—allows you to get relatively immediate and trackable feedback from your target customers. Examples of direct marketing techniques include:

- *Direct mail.* From post cards promoting new record releases to press kits promoting agency rosters, direct mail is used regularly and frequently by music people. Virtually all music people—performers, songwriters, agents, managers, and promoters—use the mail in some way (beyond routine one-to-one correspondence). Note: Direct mail includes both postal "snail mail" and e-mail.

- *Telemarketing.* Ever get a phone call from someone trying to sell you long distance service, credit card benefit programs, or newspaper subscriptions? Those are examples of using the telephone to promote a product directly to target customers. Kind of annoying, huh? Still, music people use the telephone all the time, though not in the same fashion. For example, an artist looking for an agent without personal referrals may identify prospective agents in one of the industry directories and make initial contact via telephone.

- *Cold canvassing* or *missionary selling.* Remember door-to-door sales of vacuum cleaners? That's an example of direct marketing, face to face. While not always practical, there are plenty of music industry stories about songwriters approaching artists at concerts with a "hey, please listen to my tape" pitch. Sometimes they work, but the success stories are closer to urban legends than to proven promotional methods.

To repeat a key point, the attractiveness of direct marketing as a promotional method lies in its "trackability" (results versus cost) and relatively fast feedback.

Tool 6: Trade Events

Quick review: The best kind of advertising is word of mouth, but that's not always practical. Cold canvassing gets immediate feedback and is trackable, but may also be impractical or inappropriate. Music industry trade shows, conferences, and seminars (the all-inclusive term is "trade event") represent hybrid promotional opportunities.

Trade events are definitively about business, as opposed to concerts, festivals, or other show dates, which are about providing an entertainment experience for the target audience. Depending on your overall promotional strategy, trade events may offer a cost-effective medium for reaching a group of target customers, face to face, in one location, in a relatively short period of time.

How do trade shows, conferences, and seminars differ? Aren't they essentially the same thing? Here's a quick overview:

- *Trade shows* usually last two to four days and include an exhibit hall, social activities, and educational workshops or seminars. Many music trade associations present trade shows on a regular basis.

- *Conferences* generally last one to three days and include the educational activities along with social or networking opportunities. Conferences offer multiple activities simultaneously, organized around themes or "tracks." The lack of an exhibit hall usually means that the price of admission and quality of education is higher than at trade shows.

- *Seminars and workshops* generally last one to twelve hours and focus on a single topic. The class size is often limited to allow the attendee individual access to the instructor.

Conferences and seminars are often co-located with trade shows. Here's an example. A conference promoter partners with a trade show promoter to stage a series of educational workshops in the same city, in the same convention facility or hotel, and on the same dates. Why? Because the events are relevant to the same target audience.

Why mention trade events in a chapter on promotion?

Trade event promoters look for advertising or sponsorship revenue based on the buying power and promotional value of the audience they attract.

Promoters are also eager to enrich the value of the conference, seminar, or workshop for the attendees. Your target customers may be the ones attending the event. At trade events, you have the opportunity to do the following:

- One-on-one, face-to-face promotion. You've heard the terms "networking" or "schmoozing." These are prime activities at trade events.

- Advertising. Most trade event promoters sell space in show directories, conference programs, or special-event-related publications.

- Exhibit booth. If the event is a trade show with an exhibit hall, you can "set up shop" and conduct business right on the show floor. Your booth is a place to hold meetings, present your products, and take the pulse of the event.

- Sales literature and collateral material distribution. From business cards and artist biographies to sample CDs or videos, you have the opportunity to get your materials into the hands of multiple target customers over a short period of time.

- Special event sponsorship. Special events like showcase concerts, keynote speeches, or private receptions are also promotional opportunities at most trade events. You may have the opportunity to fly a banner, distribute literature, or even speak to an assembled audience.

Tool 7: Key Influencer Relations

Influencers are people who do not buy from you, but who can influence your target customers. Here are examples of influencers, arranged by industry role:

- Performers can influence who gets booked as their opening act, who gets signed to their record labels, whose songs they record, and what other performers are handled by their agent or manager.

- Record label executives and producers can influence who gets signed to a label, what songs are recorded, what recording studios are used, and what studio musicians are hired.

- Agents and managers can influence who gets signed to record deals, who gets signed to representation agreements, and what special opportunities for exposure (television, radio, film, etc.) an artist or songwriter can get.

- Promoters can influence other promoters, record labels, agents, and managers on which artists to work with or hire again.

The point is that you need to establish and maintain relationships with anyone who can potentially have a positive influence on your target customers. This may be as simple as sending a periodic newsletter or as complicated as staging a private thank-you reception for key people. A consistent program of staying in touch can go a long way toward optimizing your other promotional activities.

Tool 8: Identity Items

Identity item is the generic term for tangible promotional gifts that include your identity (name, logo, message) and have some intrinsic value beyond pure promotion. The item is actually *useful* to the recipient. Other common names for identity items include "advertising specialties," "tschotschkes" (find that in the dictionary!), and "swag." Examples include:

- *Wearables*, ranging from the legendary T-shirt to jackets, watches, jewelry, backpacks, briefcases, lab coats, caps, gloves, underwear, or other clothing and luggage items.
- *Non-wearables*, such as CD openers, guitar picks, pens, pencils, key rings, pocket knives, clocks, sculpture, flower arrangements, plants, wall plaques, calendars, calculators, PDAs, refrigerator magnets, and desk accessories.
- *Edibles*, including candy, fruit baskets, gourmet assortments, wine, steak, chocolate-covered macadamia nuts (my favorite), or virtually any food or beverage that can accompany your promotional message or be imprinted with your identity in some way.

Music people are human beings, and they remember thoughtful gifts. The challenge is to choose appropriate items that are affordable and have the right impact. A performer's key ring with a logo on it may not land a recording deal, but it may remind promoters that the act is serious about its business and cares for its fans.

To state the obvious, some identity items are also products that can be sold to fans. Virtually all wearables and non-wearables can be merchandised at shows and through your direct marketing efforts.

Tool 9: Showcase Performances

In bygone days, there were auditions—live performances in front of someone who might hire a musician or act. These ranged from individual singers and instrumentalists vying for a spot in a band or orchestra to whole ensembles looking for club or concert bookings. These days, recordings—especially video— have streamlined the audition process. Instead of booking a hall for a day and staging a series of live auditions, a producer often pre-screens applicants via audio or video, and then interviews only the final candidates.

The audition process is somewhat different from that of a showcase performance. A showcase is an unpaid live performance with a commercial motive. Here are examples of those motives:

- Performer: Secure future bookings, close a recording deal, attract an agent or manager, build a fan base, develop an image.
- Songwriter: Place songs with recording artists, close a publishing or recording deal, attract an agent or manager.
- Agent or manager: Sponsor showcase events where multiple represented acts perform for target customers, including promoters and record labels.
- Promoter: Sponsor free or inexpensive concerts to build a fan base and expose new acts or new music genres to target audiences. Note: This is done more frequently in the not-for-profit world, but at all levels it is common to provide free show tickets to people who are prospective customers or key influencers.

Live showcases are one of the promotional tools available to you. In building your marketing plan, choose wisely the quantity and quality of unpaid gigs.

Tool 10: E-Commerce

It's been interesting to follow the development of the Internet as a music industry promotional tool. In the early days (mid-1990s), artists, agents, and record labels began using websites and e-mail lists as low-cost alternatives to sales literature and direct mail. By 2001, a website and e-mail campaign was considered essential to any music business—even that of an individual performer or songwriter.

There are three types of websites:

1. Informational. This is the most rudimentary site, sometimes called "read only" because it does not allow interaction. Informational sites are online alternatives to sales literature. You can post bios, photos, itineraries, sample contracts and riders, and sample audio or video clips. These can be viewed or downloaded by prospective customers, fans, and your competitors.

2. Interactive. This type of site generally includes the features of an informational site, but adds the ability for customers or fans to interact. The most common example is e-mail feedback. A visitor to an interactive site can send a message to you directly from within the site. Further interaction includes online forums, chat rooms, and surveys.

3. Transactional. This type of site includes the ability to conduct sales transactions online. This is especially valuable to performers, songwriters, and promoters who sell records, identity items, or tickets to the general public.

Like publicity, e-commerce can be relatively inexpensive, but it is not free. Take into account the initial production costs, online service fees, and the time it takes to keep the site fresh with new content. While not free, these costs are definable and represent a good value, especially when planned in conjunction with other promotional tools.

THREE KEY QUESTIONS ABOUT YOUR PROMOTIONAL STRATEGY

As you review the many promotional options available, you may wonder what combination of tools is best for you.

While the sheer number of promotional opportunities can be overwhelming or confusing, take comfort in knowing that you have control over your specific situation.

Here are three key questions to ask yourself as you plan the promotional link in the marketing chain:

1. Do I have to use all ten categories of promotional tools? The answer is "probably not." There is some overlap. Think of your promotional toolbox as a checklist of options, not a prescription.

2. What can I afford? The range of promotional expense budgets for most music businesses is 1% to 10% of total revenue. Some businesses spend more, some less. If you are spending less than 1% of your total revenue on promotion, you are probably not promoting enough. If you are spending more than 10%, you are either spending too much or your promotion is not working effectively.

3. What if I'm no good at writing marketing copy, graphic design, or promotional strategy? This is a big question and points to the value of building a team of people with promotional expertise. Your team can be made up of employees, freelancers, marketing service companies like ad agencies or publicists, or a combination of all three. The point is that someone needs to do the work, and if it is not you, then find someone you can pay to do it.

Note that I did not specify a dollar amount for your promotion budget, but rather a *percentage of total revenue*. It is much better to back into the promotion budget after planning total revenue than it is to commit to promotional efforts and then figure out how to pay for them.

Many music people get burned by spending too much on the wrong things in the early stages of their business. Retreating with a sour taste of the promotion world, they go too far the other way and don't use the ten tools effectively. You can prevent this problem. The checklists and templates in the Reference Section and on the CD-ROM provide a starting point for planning your promotional strategy, costs, and milestones over time.

KEY POINTS IN THIS CHAPTER

1. Promotion is the process of delivering controlled messages about you and your products to your target customers, audience, and other stakeholders. "Controlled" is a key concept here: *you* make decisions about what information to send and when.

2. Branding is the creation of indelible images of you and your products in the minds of your target customers, audience, and other stakeholders. As such, promotion helps you build your brand.

3. Advertising is often the first thing that comes to mind when people think of promotion. While advertising is a key element, it may not be appropriate for your marketing plan. You have many other choices.

4. There are ten categories of tools in your "promotional toolbox." They are (1) advertising, (2) publicity, (3) sales literature, (4) demo recordings and other collateral materials, (5) direct marketing, (6) trade events, (7) key influencer relations, (8) identity items, (9) showcase performances, and (10) e-commerce.

5. Many music businesses rely heavily on publicity, demo recordings, identity items, showcase performances, and e-commerce.

6. Your promotional mix will depend on your unique set of marketing and sales objectives, budget, and capacity to implement your promotional strategy. You do not need to use tools in all ten categories.

7. Budget 1% to 10% of your total revenue for promotional expenses. While some music businesses may spend more or less, start here for planning purposes.

8. Someone needs to do the promotional work. Options include yourself, your employees, freelancers, ad agencies, publicists, or a combination.

9. Be prepared to use the Internet as a promotional tool. Virtually all music businesses are expected to have websites and e-mail capability.

CHAPTER TWELVE

YOUR PLACE OF BUSINESS

The fourth link in the marketing chain involves the physical environment in which business is conducted. The marketing textbooks call this "place," or the "fourth p," after product, pricing, and promotion. In this chapter we will discuss three aspects of place and how they relate to your marketing strategy.

WHY PLACE IS A MARKETING STRATEGY

Where you conduct business has an impact on all the other links in the marketing chain. These are the three dimensions of place to consider: (1) geographical territory, (2) *channel of distribution* or venue type, and (3) your workspace—office, studio, or other day-to-day business headquarters.

Now that we are into the fourth link in the marketing chain, we'll start to see how all of the links work together. Sometimes this gets a little murky. Is a venue type also a target customer? If I broker show dates through a subsidiary agent, is that a separate channel, part of my salesforce, or also a target customer? If I'm an independent promoter, do the venues I use represent customers or channels?

We'll address the answers to these questions in this chapter and in Chapters Thirteen and Fourteen. For now, here are the key points:

- You decide where you want to work.
- Your decision has three dimensions: geographical, channel/venue, and workspace.
- The strategy changes over time.
- Place is a marketing strategy because it has an impact on all the other links in the marketing chain.

Let's look at the three dimensions one at a time.

Place Dimension 1: Geographical Territory

Where do your customers live and do business? Is it just in your community, or the whole world? The geography that you cover is called your "trade area." The options are:

- Local—your community and surrounding area

- Regional—several states or provinces

- National—the whole country

- International—more than one country (Note: International often implies more than one continent, like North America plus Europe.)

- Global—everywhere worldwide

- Interplanetary—coming soon

For some music people, the prestige of trading nationally or internationally is compelling. For others it's scary or unnecessary. For example, if you are a part-time performer with a day job, it is not practical to be a national act. Or, if you are a full-time performer with long-term career plans, you may start regionally and branch out over time as you develop an audience.

If you are a songwriter, agent, or manager, the practical aspects are a little simpler to handle. You do not need to physically go to every venue to perform in order to get paid. Still, the element of *focus* enters into the strategy. Can you develop and maintain customer relationships over a wide area? Understanding time zones, foreign languages, and different business cultures becomes critical to your success, because all are driven by your geographical territory decisions.

The same holds true for event promoters. While networks of regional and national promoters emerged in the late 1990s, the majority of events—private, corporate, civic, etc.—are handled by local independent promoters.

Place Dimension 2: Channel or Venue Type

"Channel of distribution" is the business term for the type of venue where you work or sell products. Consider a manufacturer selling consumer electronics equipment, from boom boxes to high-end home theaters. The manufacturer has several choices of "dealer channels": superstores, independent specialty retailers, boutiques, or systems contractors. Which channel is appropriate depends on the product, the pricing, and the rest of the strategic marketing links presented in this book.

There are, of course, parallels in music. It's easy to plug record sales into the example above. Records are sold everywhere from supermarkets and convenience stores to web-based specialty retailers. The record label chooses the channel or combination of channels that optimizes sales, manages expenses, and sends the right positioning message to the market.

Consider the following examples:

- Performers target venues by size and format. These range from small coffeehouses and private residences to clubs, colleges, large arenas, stadiums, and outdoor festivals. Which one you choose depends on the style of music, the target audience, your act's drawing power, and the positioning statement that you want to make.

- Songwriters pitch songs to publishing companies, record labels, producers, managers, and to artists directly. Each of these represent a channel toward the ultimate goal; that is, to get songs recorded and performed publicly. Songwriters and composers may choose to specialize in a specific performance format like records, film, or television. This decision has an impact on the channel as well.

- Agents sell acts directly to venues, to show producers, or through other agents. The choice may depend on the act represented and the other strategies as discussed. While on one hand a venue or event producer is a target customer, the channel decision has other dimensions. For example, an agent who books on the local or regional level may affiliate with other regional or national agencies to optimize touring opportunities for an emerging national act.

- Managers sell acts to agents, producers, record labels, and promoters. The manager decides whether to use a single agent or multiple agencies depending on the performer's specific situation and needs. Also, managers influence their artists on what types of venues to play and when. This points to the need for a clear channel/venue strategy agreed to by each party (manager, agent, performer).

As a manager, should I use an outside agent, or play the role of agent myself? The answer relates partly to the channel strategy and partly to the profile of the salesforce as discussed in Chapter Thirteen.

- Promoters make venue and channel decisions as well. The range of venue choices parallels that of performers: clubs, concert halls, and the full spectrum of alternative performance spaces. Promoters sell tickets through venue box offices, ticket bureaus and brokers, mail order, and online.

Are you a club promoter or a concert promoter? Do you work exclusively with specific venues, or nonexclusively with many venues? Do you copromote with other firms? Are you tied to a local radio station for promotion? These are all examples of channel or venue strategies. The answer is often all of the above and depends on the specific type of show, location, performers, and promotional considerations.

Place Dimension 3: Your Workspace

The term "workspace" refers to the place where you do what you do on a regular basis. Here I am referring to offices, recording studios, and rehearsal halls, as opposed to performance venues. Many music people work at home. Others work on the road—in cars and vans, hotel rooms, restaurants, and airport boarding lounges. While this decision is often driven by practical concerns, it is your choice nonetheless.

Workspaces need to have certain basic elements in order to be viable. For all music people those elements include:

- Access to communication tools: telephone, fax, Internet connection
- Access to files and business records
- Access to reference materials
- Privacy
- Comfort
- Storage space for everything from instruments and stage gear to promotional materials and merchandise

These are operational issues as opposed to marketing strategies. From a marketing standpoint, your workspace needs the following:

- Enough space to conduct any necessary meetings
- Décor and amenities that are pleasant for you and anyone who meets with you at your workspace
- A location that is secure yet easy to find; parking may also be a consideration
- A location in a part of town which is consistent with the image you want to project

Here are some examples:

- Performers need a place at home for computer, instruments, equipment, and business records. Depending on your family situation, this may be a separate room or part of the garage or basement. Rehearsals can be held at home or a designated rehearsal space, depending on the nature of the act.
- Songwriters and composers generally need to record what they are writing. Their physical workspace may be a home studio, an office away from home, or a commercial recording studio.
- Agents, managers, and promoters may need less space for storing gear, but often need more space for customer meetings and storage of business records and materials. Business offices range from small rooms at home to shared space in office suites to customized office buildings.

The Pros and Cons of Home Offices

Do I need plush offices in the high-rent district? Can I work from a desk in my spare room? Does it matter?

The answers to these questions do matter to both you and your customers. Like the other two dimensions of place, the characteristics of your workspace will change over time. Try to think of your workspace as part of your marketing strategy in addition to the purely practical or operational considerations.

Where you work from and what the surroundings are like say a lot about you and your business. Thankfully, the home-office revolution started in the late 1980s is still going on today. There is little or no stigma attached to working from a home office—as long as it has the facilities and resources required to do the job.

Advantages of home offices include:

- Relatively low cost. Assuming you have space, you do not need to incur extra rent, utilities, or insurance expenses to operate from home.

- Convenience. The "20-foot commute" is enviable, especially if the alternative is sitting in traffic for long periods every day.

- Amenities. It's nice to have all the comforts of home at your fingertips.

Disadvantages of home offices include:

- Distractions. Your household situation (family, roommates, etc.) may not allow you the privacy required to focus on your business.

- Logistics. Your residence may be too hard for others to find, or too small for you to conduct business.

- Possible zoning problems. It may be illegal to conduct business from your home—check local laws governing commercial versus residential zones. Note: This generally applies only to businesses that have employees or customers coming and going on a regular basis.

Regardless of where your workspace is, remember that it is a part of your marketing strategy and will change as your business needs change.

YOUR EVOLVING PLACE STRATEGY

A quick review: A strategy is a decision that affects future activity. How does your future business strategy have an impact on place: geography, channel/venue, and workspace? Do you always want to perform in small listening rooms, or do you see yourself (or the acts you represent) moving up to larger venues?

Remember that there are no right or wrong answers to these questions. What you do evolves as your business strategy changes over time.

KEY POINTS IN THIS CHAPTER

1. Where you conduct business has an impact on your overall marketing strategy.

2. "Place" has three dimensions: (1) geographical territory, (2) channel or venue, and (3) personal workspace.

3. Geographical territories can be local, regional, national, international, or global.

4. Channel of distribution is a term that comes from manufacturing but is relevant to any place strategy. You choose the channel and/or type of venue where you plan to work.

5. Performance venue types range from private residences to clubs, colleges, arenas, stadiums, and festivals.

6. Examples of channels for services may include producers, record labels, promoters, or other agents or managers.

7. Examples of channels for goods include record stores, bookstores, performance venue concession stands, mail order, or Internet retailers.

8. Workspaces have practical elements, such as access to tools and privacy, as well as positioning elements, such as size and location. Home offices have both advantages and disadvantages for music people.

9. Like other links in the marketing chain, your place strategy changes over time. Your business plan helps you anticipate those changes and moves.

CHAPTER THIRTEEN

PORTRAIT OF A SALESFORCE

Now let's look at your salesforce strategy—the fifth link in the marketing chain. Your salesforce is the person or persons who handle your business's sales functions as described in Chapter Eight. As with the other marketing links, your salesforce strategy evolves over time. We'll suggest how to optimize the fit of the salesforce to the product by creating a profile of the ideal salesperson.

EVERYONE PLAYS A SALES ROLE

Regardless of your product or your role in the music industry, you are involved in sales—whether you like it or not. Agents and promoters tend to be natural salespeople. They chose those roles because they enjoy them. Performers and songwriters may be less likely to enjoy the role of salesperson, and often delegate sales responsibility to an agent or manager. Managers—while often responsible for sales—are in between agent and performer in terms of their proclivity for sales.

Everyone sells something at some point.

- Performers need to sell themselves to agents, managers, and producers in order to get work. Many performers also represent themselves for live performance bookings, and actively play an ongoing sales role in addition to the performer role.

- Songwriters sell their songs to artists, publishers, record producers, and record label people. Music publishers play a sales role on behalf of songwriters, analogous to the agent/performer relationship. Still, songwriters need basic sales skills to get in the door with a publishing firm or record producer.

- Agents sell acts to event promoters. This is the most direct connection between an industry role and the concept of a salesforce. In addition, agents sell their services to the performers they represent.

- Managers sell performers to agents and producers. Like agents, they also sell their services to performers. Some managers also play the agent/salesperson role and sell directly to promoters and venues.

- Promoters sell tickets and shows to the general public. Like agents, promoters are full-time sales and marketing people. They also sell their company capabilities to venues, agents, managers, and performers.

WHAT IF I DON'T LIKE THE IDEA OF SALES?

Many music people associate sales with a negative stereotype image. Even the word "salesman" conjures an image of an overweight, middle-aged huckster with ill-fitting clothes, bad breath, and worse jokes. Or, sensationalized stories of music people getting burned by "business types" or "suits" come to mind. Everyone has heard a horror story, and unfortunately, many of them are true.

Sales is not a necessary evil. It is a positive process and the lifeblood of any business, music or otherwise. Consider this old expression:

"Nothing happens until somebody sells something."

That "something" can be your idea or your product. If you don't like the idea of sales—for whatever personal reasons—you have to make a choice. Here are the options:

1. Hang in there and handle sales even though it might not be your favorite thing to do.

2. Have someone who enjoys sales handle it for you.

3. Go out of business, or don't go into business in the first place.

Clearly, option #2 is the best choice. Thankfully, there are many people out there who are good at selling and enjoy the process. The challenge is to find someone who loves to sell and also loves your product.

A WORD ABOUT INTEGRITY

It is assumed that any qualified salesperson operates legally and ethically. There is no subjective rating scale for these items. A salesperson's integrity is essential for business success. Infractions are grounds for the salesperson's disqualification or termination.

Regrettably, the music industry is replete with examples of unwitting performers and songwriters being taken advantage of by unscrupulous opportunists. Once again, the popular media consistently present attorneys, agents, pitchmen, and "corporate" types as unscrupulous money-mongers, who will to stop at nothing to get rich at innocent musicians' expense.

Fraud and extortion happen in all industries. Music people, like other creative and technical types, may be more susceptible to deception or more likely to become the victims of unfair dealing than people in other business categories.

It doesn't need to be that way. The clear majority of people in the music industry—both in the corporate and in the independent world—are honest, sincere, "normal" folks. Too often, however, they lack fundamental business skills and have a poor understanding of the sales process. (But they don't necessarily have malicious or criminal intent.) A corporate title and a few years of experience do not guarantee that the person is qualified. You are helping to prevent problems and misunderstandings by reading this book.

CHARACTERISTICS OF A GREAT SALESPERSON—THE "THREE C'S"

Great sales people have a group of basic qualities that are essential to sales success. Your sales representatives need strength in the "three c's of sales": competence, capacity, and chemistry.

1. Competence: the business skills and experience to do the job. These include product knowledge, market knowledge, time management, presentation and negotiation skills, accuracy of communications, speedy follow-through on all matters, and general business acumen.

2. Capacity: time, people, tools, and resources to achieve your sales objectives. This refers to number of sales and support persons, computer and telecommunications tools, manageable number of products represented, and ability to cover the assigned geographic territory.

3. Chemistry: the human interface. This refers to the subjective yet vitally important aspects of business relationships including courtesy, attitude, patience, adaptability, sense of humor, and shared vision.

These elements are the basis for evaluating how any individual or firm will fit with your company. Competence and capacity issues can be rated relatively objectively. Chemistry is more subjective and will vary depending on who is doing the evaluation.

THE IDEAL SALES REP

Your salesforce—whoever represents you and handles sales functions—needs to be strong in each of the key areas of competence, capacity, and chemistry. Here is a detailed profile of the ideal sales representative.

Competence

1. Product and music industry knowledge. Understands your product categories and how they fit into the overall music industry. For example, your agent has seen your act perform and can characterize it properly, now and into the future.

2. Knowledge of your target market. Has experience dealing with the kind of customers that you want to reach. Knows who the major industry influencers and buyers are and how to do business with them. Understands the relevance and workings of music trade associations, from NARAS and the AFM to local music societies that stage concerts and festivals.

3. Time management ability. Makes the best use of staff time in developing new business and expediting solutions to problems and opportunities.

4. Solid organization and presentation skills. Able to present you and your product faithfully to customers. Respects individual customer's schedules and buying patterns.

5. Marketing skills. Able to assist customers with publicity and general promotion. Interfaces comfortably with key market influencers on behalf of you and your company.

6. Communication skills. Able to communicate accurately with proper attention to detail in completion of proposals, contracts, forecasts, and reports. Able to send and receive information dependably.

7. Timeliness. Performs speedy follow-up on all routine tasks and special assignments. Works well within deadlines.

8. General business knowledge. Understands how business is conducted in the music industry and beyond. Includes working knowledge of sales, marketing, finance, information systems, and management.

Capacity

1. Proper ratio of sales staff to clients. The individual or firm must be able to dedicate adequate sales staff time to all clients or projects represented.

2. Access to a real live office person for both clients and customers. There is generally so much for an agency or promotion company to do that a full-time office person is a necessity. Agents, managers, and other salespersons are most effective face to face with customers, knowing they have support at the office.

3. Business equipment. Computer, fax machine, and telephone are minimum tools. As the company grows over time, the equipment needs also grow and change. Make sure that your salesforce has the right gear.

4. Growth plans and adaptability. The person or firm needs to grow and be able to adapt to the changing music market. The best firms have a business plan and are willing to discuss their long-term strategy with their clients.

5. Training and ongoing education. Willing and able to take the time needed to learn about new products, programs, and business procedures. As a performer, for example, you may want to branch out into a new market (like state fairs or corporate meetings). Your salesforce, then, must have the time and ability—the capacity—to learn about the new market before leaping ahead.

Chemistry

1. Positive attitude. This is expressed consistently toward clients, customers, and the music industry in general. No one wants to buy from a jerk or a sourpuss.

2. Telephone manners and efficiency. So much sales work is done over the phone that it is essential that the salesperson come across as friendly, sincere, and respectful.

3. Tactfulness. We'll allow for variations in personal style, but the salesperson should be able to deliver good news and bad news in a professional manner.

4. Congruent quality image. Your products are top quality and marketed to special customers. The salesforce's image needs to be consistent with you and your product's image.

5. Shared vision of the future. Your salesforce needs to know and believe in your goals and objectives. This is perhaps the most important chemistry-oriented characteristic of the ideal salesperson. The best reps see the full potential for your products and will invest time and energy to help you realize that potential. If your rep does not take you seriously, move on!

WHAT GREAT SALESPEOPLE LOOK FOR IN A MUSIC PRODUCT

Great salespeople keep both their clients' and customers' interests in mind. For example, a good agent wants to keep performers and promoters or venue owners happy and coming back for more.

It is also essential that the salesperson be positively motivated on a consistent basis. In other words, everybody needs to win in the course of a business relationship.

To that end, it is important to understand what salespeople look for in the products they represent. Here are five characteristics of an excellent product, from the salesperson's point of view:

1. Excellent quality. Whether selling live show dates, songs, tickets, merchandise, or services, the product needs to be of the highest quality. That way the salesperson can stake his or her reputation on it with confidence.

2. Longevity. The better established the product, the easier it is to sell. This has a future dimension as well. Salespeople will invest more time developing the market for a product that has a long life ahead of it.

3. Professional commitment. While this should go without saying, it needs to be said. Too many music people are unclear or noncommittal about their professional music career. Good agents and managers ask about commitment in initial interviews. They can sense when an artist is or is not ready to be a professional.

4. Marketability. A good salesperson needs to know what your target market or customer is. They also need to understand and believe in the fit between your product and your customer base.

5. Financial viability. The salesforce needs to get paid, so they need to understand and believe in your product's commercial potential. Remember, everyone has their own idea of how much money is enough. There needs to be congruity between your financial objectives and those of your salesforce.

What if any of these five elements are lacking? Experienced agents, managers, publishers, and record people simply will not take on performers or songwriters who don't have market potential or are not ready, willing, and able to make a professional commitment. Your marketing plan goes a long way toward attracting the best people to your salesforce.

On the other hand, inexperienced salespeople (like the proverbial friend of the band) may mistake talent and sincerity for your act's business potential. They may become discouraged quickly when they discover that key elements of your business are lacking or undefined.

It's better to avoid asking friends and family to sell for you unless they have the basic characteristics of competence, capacity, and chemistry. "But it's a labor of love," they might say. What happens when something more important comes along, like their full-time job, or it's time to take the kids to soccer practice? You may be better off representing yourself until your "product" is ready for professional representation.

KEY POINTS IN THIS CHAPTER

1. Everyone—performers, songwriters, agents, managers, and promoters alike—gets involved in the sales process in some way.

2. If you don't like the idea of sales, that's OK. You can choose to (1) tough it out on your own, (2) delegate sales to someone else like an agent, or (3) go out of business.

3. You can't run a business without sales! It is the lifeblood of any music business—no one gets paid without it. Remember the axiom, "Nothing happens until somebody sells something."

4. Great salespeople have complete integrity. Beware of media stereotypes portraying slick or unscrupulous opportunists feeding on the weaknesses of unsophisticated music people.

5. Great salespeople have balanced strength in the "three c's" of sales: competence (business skills), capacity (resources), and chemistry (positive personality traits).

6. Great salespeople represent great products. They look for five primary characteristics: (1) excellent quality, (2) longevity, (3) professional commitment, (4) marketability, and (5) financial viability.

7. If any of these are weak or lacking, the fit between your product and your salesforce may be compromised.

8. Beware of inexperienced salespeople—like friends and family members—who are willing to work for you despite a lack of marketability or long-term financial viability.

9. Your marketing plan will go a long way toward attracting the best sales people.

10. You are better off doing the selling yourself than using representation that's wrong for you.

CHAPTER FOURTEEN

THE WHO, WHAT, WHEN, WHERE, WHY, AND HOW OF YOUR CUSTOMERS

Here we come to the sixth link in the marketing chain: customers. We'll outline how to create customer profiles and how to apply them to your marketing plan.

First, a quick review. In Chapter Two we identified the need to understand who your customers are—even before you go into business. Here are those three key strategic questions again:

- What's the business or product?

- What's the market or target customer?

- How does everyone get paid?

We also offered a simple definition of a customer: the one who pays for your product. In other words, your relationship with your customers helps determine where the money changes hands.

UNDERSTANDING BUYER CHARACTERISTICS

Whoever pays you for your product—your customer—has a set of identifiable characteristics. It is this set of characteristics that makes up a *customer profile*. The elements of the profile include:

- *Demographic information.* Demographics include age, gender, marital status, and education level. For example, a "boy band" may target 11- to 15–year-old female high school students. An opera company or symphony may target college-educated men and women age 35 and older. An agent may choose to represent only unmarried performers due to the rigors of travel and the impact of touring on home life.

- *Economic information.* This includes household income levels and discretionary spending ability, or *buying power.* For example, some people will pay up to $15 for a concert ticket or record while others can afford $100 or more. On a *business-to-business* level—like agents selling acts to promoters—the economic portion of the profile is where you identify the budget range of your target customer. For example, a 300-seat club with a $1,000 budget for a main act is unlikely to book a $20,000 auditorium act. Nor would it book a $250 coffeehouse act who might not draw enough to fill the room.

- *Geographic information.* Where do your customers physically live? This element is most important to performers and promoters. The smaller the geographic "trade area" the easier it is to focus and control costs like travel and promotion. You can be a local, regional, national, international, or global act or promoter. For songwriters, agents, and managers, there is greater flexibility in the geographic location of your customers. Most business can be conducted via telephone, e-mail, and at occasional trade events. Still, you may decide that your target customers live and work in a specific area that is music-friendly or where the population of music people is denser, such as Los Angeles, New York, Nashville, Chicago, Miami, Austin, Vancouver, Toronto, and other focal points for music performing, recording, and publishing.

- *Psychographic information.* Psychographics have to do with what your customers think about and believe. This includes social traits, religious or spiritual beliefs, political views, and hobbies or personal interests. For example, a topical songwriter may target recording artists, labels, and publishers who accept and specialize in socio-political material. Gospel musicians may target specific church denominations that are more receptive to their musical message. Agents and managers may choose to represent artists whose lifestyle and political views are compatible with their own. Promoters may choose to present acts they believe in to audiences who are receptive to a specific style of music.

A WORD ABOUT STYLE: THE BLUES BROTHERS EXAMPLE

The psychographic element is the one that music people often think of first. Why? Because it relates to style or genre of music. What separates country from bluegrass? Rock from rockabilly? Jazz from blues? Folk from world? Classical from avant garde? Stylistic differences are relevant not only to the audience, but to performers, songwriters, agents, managers, and promoters. Those differences include not only the sound of the music and the look of the performers and audience, but the interests and values of everyone involved.

Remember the movie *The Blues Brothers*? Whether you've seen it or not, you can imagine this scene:

A blues band shows up for a booking at Bob's Country Bunker, a roadhouse tavern that normally features country acts. During the band's first number, the crowd—expecting their favorite style of country music—throws beer bottles at the band members. Thank goodness there was floor-to-ceiling chicken wire in front of the stage...

In the movie, it's pretty funny. In real life, it's pathetic. The business lesson is this. Understand what your target customer's interests and values are—before you make the sales pitch. The problems inherent in the Blues Brothers story can generally be prevented by creating a customer profile in advance and using it as a guiding element in the marketing mix. It is relatively common to organize everything about a music business around a style, or narrow range of styles, of music.

BUYING HABITS AND PREFERENCES

How do your target customers like to buy? Do they have special needs, habits, or preferences? The answers to these questions are additional elements in your target customer profile. The examples that follow, while not an exhaustive list, will give you ideas of what to look for.

- If your band plays weddings, be prepared to commit to future dates far in advance. The ability to guarantee that the act will show up on time, look good, and perform the right material a year from now is a set of purchase criteria that transcends demographics, economics, geography, and style.

- Promoters may choose to only book acts that they have seen in person. Be prepared to audition live, play a showcase gig for little or no money, or invite and transport the promoter to see you at another venue—or don't work for that promoter. Remember that you always have a choice.

- Music publishers and record producers have established criteria for how to submit material: number of songs, recording format, or even time of year that they are open to submissions.

- Agents and managers may or may not be seeking new acts to represent. If they are, find out what the criteria might be for submitting your act for consideration.

- Promoters may have a geographical limit on dates booked in competitive venues. For example, if you (as a performer) or your act (as agent or manager) are looking for a show date within a specific time frame, you may have to guarantee that the promoter has an exclusive within a 50-mile radius plus or minus 30 days.

These are examples of special buying criteria or characteristics. There are two business points here. First, understand your customer's buying habits. Second, incorporate positive criteria—the ones you can live with—in the profile of your target customer.

INDIVIDUAL VS. INSTITUTIONAL CUSTOMERS

Another important aspect of customer profiling is to understand who actually makes the buying decision. Is it a single person or a group? Does the person you are selling to have the authority to make the commitment, or does it require a vote or blessing by someone else? In this context, there are two types of customers: individual and institutional.

Individual customers make the decision to buy on their own and are usually spending their own money. Examples include:

- Clubs or other venues where the owner books the acts
- Independent record labels or publishing companies run by the owner
- The general public when they buy show tickets or records

Institutional customers make buying decisions in groups and are often spending an organization's money. Examples include:

- College and university "activities committees"
- Major corporate record labels and publishing companies
- Ticket brokers and resellers

Is one type of customer better or worse than the other? That depends on your ability to deal with the special circumstances—buying preferences and characteristics—inherent in each situation. The point is to be aware that each of the two types of customers behave differently, have different buying criteria, and need to be marketed and sold to differently as a result.

WHAT ABOUT NONVIABLE CUSTOMERS?

As you develop your target customer profile, you are likely to think of the bad examples along with the good—the proverbial "customers from hell." When you identify the buying criteria that you can't live with—the "deal-breakers"—you are creating a profile of a nonviable customer. This is a valuable exercise.

Many music people think that they have to live with bad customer relationships as part of "paying your dues" in the music industry. While there is some value in living through challenging experiences, most music people learn the hard way by trial and error and either move on or get out of the business. Understanding your own tolerances and comparing them to your customer profiles helps prevent problems and optimizes results.

HOW TO SLICE THE PIE

Your customers can be organized into natural segments. Think of a segment as a "slice of the orange" or a "piece of the pie." Market segmentation, as it's called in the business world, is the process of organizing your approach to target your customers for the sake of focus and efficiency.

If you define your target audience as "all music lovers" or "all buyers of talent," where do you start? How do you know if your publicity and collateral material are on target? How do you know who to call first? The idea is to narrow the focus to a group of prospective customers who (1) you understand, (2) have demonstrated interest in your type of product, and (3) are targetable from a communications standpoint.

Let's talk about *targetable* a little more. Targeting involves reaching out to current and prospective customers via telephone, e-mail, websites, trade shows, and the media as described in Chapter Eleven. Remember that your customers are not likely to come after you. You need to go after them. To that end, do you start with the local phone book and start calling everyone, or use an industry directory to narrow the focus? Using a prequalified list of prospective customers is much more efficient and potentially rewarding.

As we discussed earlier in this chapter, the music industry is oriented towards styles or genres of music. That often becomes the first market segmentation principle. The other principles flow naturally from the remaining categories of customer information: demographic, economic, geographic, and psychographic. When you segment your market, you not only focus on customers who are attractive to your business, but you also intentionally avoid unqualified or unattractive customers. That's where efficiency kicks in.

For most music people this is intuitive and simple to understand. You might be thinking, "I'm already focusing on my genre of music in a geographical area that makes sense to me right now." Any performer, agent, or manager who has traveled to a distant gig where the venue and audience was expecting something else (like Bob's Country Bunker) knows what I mean.

Yet, it is tempting to take that festival or college booking four states over, even though you will lose money due to the time and travel expenses involved. Your options are to work the date and pay the price or respectfully decline the offer, citing the current geographical focus of your act. Most promoters understand the rationale and will keep the door open to discuss future work as your business grows and your trade area expands. Just remember that you have a choice.

Here's another marketing rule of thumb: You can only focus on one or two segments at a time with any degree of efficiency. If you are trying to "walk the walk and talk the talk" of too many types of customers at one time, things can get out of hand. The exception is an organization with multiple products and the capacity to focus each product on a limited number of customer segments simultaneously, such as:

- Booking agencies or management companies representing acts in multiple musical genres
- Publishing companies representing crossover songwriters in numerous musical styles
- Promoters who present multiple musical styles to multiple audience profiles

DEVELOPING YOUR TARGET CUSTOMER PROFILE

Let's turn this all into an exercise. Take a few minutes now to write the "five-bullet" profile of your target customer. In the boxes below, there is space to add a few words to describe your customer in each of the main parameters we have presented in this chapter. Notice that there is a column for nonviable customer characteristics too. You'll find that the process of profiling both viable and noviable customers at the same time is both illuminating and liberating. Note: This exercise is also included on the CD-ROM so you can complete it as many times as you need to. For now, start with one product and one target customer type and see how it goes.

Customer Profiling Exercise

Profile Element	Viable Customer	Nonviable Customer
Musical genre or style		
Demographic information		
Economic information		
Geographic information		
Psychographic information		
Special buying criteria		

DON'T LET YOUR DEAL-BREAKERS PUT YOU OUT OF BUSINESS

We mentioned the concept of deal-breakers earlier—the criteria that make a customer nonviable to you. You've just listed a few in the exercise above. The point of mentioning it again is this: Beware of having so narrow a focus that there are not enough customers to support your business. For example, let's say that you are a performer and your target customer profile is "left-handed heart surgeons who love zydeco music and are willing to pay $50,000 for a private performance." If you find one, let me know. If you find enough to make a sustainable living, it's a miracle.

While that may be an extreme example, I encourage you to apply the thought process to your own situation. By going through the profiling exercise several times, you'll find the balance between the ideal and the practical and be able to proceed from there.

KEY POINTS IN THIS CHAPTER

1. The sixth link in the marketing chain is understanding customers. A customer is the one who pays for your product, or "where the money changes hands."

2. Customers have identifiable characteristics that can be organized into a *customer profile.* The four main categories of customer characteristics are demographic, economic, geographic, and psychographic.

3. Demographic information includes age, gender, marital status, and education level. You need customers who are consistent with your preferences or needs in these areas.

4. Economic information includes income, buying power, and budget guidelines. You need customers who can afford the price of your product.

5. Geographic information means where the customer physically lives or conducts business. You need customers who are in your trade area.

6. Psychographic information refers to what customers think about and believe: their social traits, religious beliefs, political views, and hobbies or personal interests. You need customers who find your product consistent with their own interests and values.

7. Each customer also has a definable set of buying criteria, habits, and preferences, such as preferred modes of communication, timing, or capacity guidelines.

8. There are two basic types of customers: individual and institutional. Individual customers make the decision to buy on their own and are often spending their own money. Institutional customers make buying decisions in groups and are often spending an organization's money.

9. As you develop profiles of target customers, you will identify "deal-breakers" or characteristics that make some customers nonviable to you. This valuable exercise helps you prevent problems.

10. Market segmentation—or slicing the pie—is the process of organizing your approach to target your customers for the sake of focus and efficiency.

11. Customer profiles in the music industry generally include musical style or genre preference as an organizing principle. By starting there and adding demographic, economic, geographic, and psychographic information, you can quickly develop profiles of target customers that enhance your marketing plan.

12. Savvy marketers focus on one or two market segments or customer profiles at a time. It is difficult and inefficient to be all things to "all music lovers" or "all buyers of talent."

13. Conversely, beware of establishing customer profiles that are so narrow you don't have enough qualified buyers to support your business.

14. You can't make a sale without a customer. Understanding in advance the purchase criteria of various customer types or segments saves you time, money, and headaches.

CHAPTER FIFTEEN

UNDERSTANDING YOUR COMPETITION

The seventh and final link in the marketing chain is the competitive analysis. In this chapter we'll target the competition and learn how to understand the competitive environment. We'll identify who your competitors are and provide tools for understanding their strengths and weaknesses.

THE COMPETITIVE ENVIRONMENT

Your competitors have one key characteristic in common: They are going after the same target customer as you are. As we discussed in Chapter Three, there are two basic kinds of competition: direct and indirect. Here's a quick review of the definitions:

- **Direct competition:** similar businesses in your product category
- **Indirect competition:** any product that goes after the same target customer's attention and money

The total competitive environment includes both the direct and indirect competitors. While this may seem obvious, I've found that most music people focus primarily on one or the other. Consider the following two scenarios.

Scenario 1: "Oh, music people are all in it together—we're one big happy family. It's sports and other leisure activities we need to worry about." This is both idealistic and unrealistic. Other performers, songwriters, agents, managers, and promoters are going after your target customers all the time and may not view you as "family."

Scenario 2: "If people aren't interested in music, I don't care about them. My problem is that there are so many performers [or songwriters, agents, managers, or promoters] going after my customers." This narrow view is also unrealistic. Who do you know that is not interested in music in some way? While sports fans may spend more on game tickets than concert tickets, that does not mean they are completely out of the market. Why do you think the half-time show at the Super Bowl features music?

Sure, these are generalized examples, but how close to real are they for you? Too many music people focus only on one type of competition—usually direct—

to the exclusion of the other. We need to focus on both in order to fully understand the competitive environment.

IDENTIFYING YOUR DIRECT COMPETITORS

It's tempting to oversimplify when identifying your direct competitors. If you are a performing songwriter, you might conclude that *all* other performing songwriters are competing for the same gigs. Likewise with agents, managers, or promoters. In a general or abstract way, that's true. However, remember the concept of the "customer profile" in Chapter Fourteen? We saw many different customer profiles, which allow you to target your direct competitors much more accurately. Consider these examples:

- You are a concert promoter who specializes in promoting rock and dance bands in clubs and theaters in a five-county area surrounding your home metropolitan area. Other promoters who focus on different styles of music (like classical, folk, or gospel), different target audiences, or different geographical areas are only marginally competing with you.

- You are a manager seeking a recording contract for an alternative country act who performs all original material and tours internationally. You focus your efforts on record labels who are known to record similar acts. While those similar acts and their managers are indeed direct competitors, a manager representing a techno/ambient act is likely to focus on a different set of labels while looking for a record deal.

- You are a pop cover band looking for "general business" or "casual" gigs: weddings, proms, private parties, and retail promotions within a 100-mile radius of where you live. Your direct competitors include similar local bands and mobile disc jockeys, but not touring acts looking for showcase clubs or concert work in your trade area.

While it is idealistic to think that all music people are "in it together" and not in competition, it is illuminating—even essential—to understand potential competitors' target customers. That is the first step in developing a competitive strategy.

UNDERSTANDING INDIRECT COMPETITION

Let's go back to the sports versus music example. Local sports teams are competing with music promoters for both ticket sales and audience attention. In addition to distracting fans, they tie up the press and may even make venues unavailable. This has an impact on the performers, agents, and managers involved, too. In other words, the impact of indirect competition crosses over music industry roles.

If a fan spends three hours and $30 on a basketball or football game, he or she did not spend that time and money on a concert, club date, or record purchase.

The same can be said of other entertainment forms, including movies, theater, museums, dance, reading, games, and comedy.

There are many additional nonentertainment types of indirect competition. Here are examples of indirect competitors who target the general public as the customer:

- Hobbies and leisure activities—from coin collecting to balloon rides
- Educational pursuits—from sending kids to private schools (using up discretionary funds) to enrolling in seminars or continuing education programs
- Home improvements—from buying furniture and appliances to adding rooms or remodeling
- Vacation travel—from camping to cruises
- Health and fitness activities—from exercise to extreme sports

These activities take lots of time and money. Similarly, there are many kinds of indirect competitors who target businesses or institutional customers. They may distract your target customer in different ways. For example:

- A company who had traditionally hired a band for its holiday party may cancel the event altogether and give employees a cash bonus instead. The competition is not another act, agent, or promoter, but something else.
- Computer hardware, software, and systems providers may distract or prevent a corporate client from using music at its annual sales meeting. The competition is not another act or agent, but time and money spent on a completely different set of activities.
- A record label may be in the process of being sold to one of the majors and forced to put a freeze on signing new acts until the deal is done. The competition is not other managers trying to place their clients, but time and legal fees spent on the acquisition.

EXERCISE: IDENTIFY YOUR TOP FIVE DIRECT AND INDIRECT COMPETITORS

By now you have a feel for how to identify competitors. Let's put that knowledge to work. In the space below, write down the names of your top five direct and indirect competitors. Note: A similar template is included in the Reference Section and on the CD-ROM.

Top Five Direct Competitors

1. _____

2. _____

3. _____

4. _____

5. _____

Top Five Indirect Competitors

1. _____

2. _____

3. _____

4. _____

5. _____

WHY INDIRECT COMPETITION IS SCARIER THAN DIRECT COMPETITION

Now look at the two lists above. How do you feel about each? Most people find the indirect competitors to be more mysterious and intimidating—*scarier*—than the direct competitors. This is true in any category of business, not just the music industry.

Many business people view their direct competitors as predictable and vulnerable; nuisances as opposed to threats. Yet the indirect competitors, like the National Football League (sports), the City of Paris, France (tourism), or Microsoft (computer software) can cause real competitive anxiety.

A typical response is, "Yikes! My direct competitors are tough enough to deal with, but these others are just overwhelming."

Why is this the case? No mystery here. It's because indirect competitors are often large, capable, and able to distract our target customers with power and consistency. The point is to recognize and learn to deal with *both* (direct and indirect competition) as part of your overall marketing plan.

COMPETITIVE STRENGTHS, WEAKNESSES, OPPORTUNITIES, AND THREATS

So what do we do about competition? How can we determine where we stand relative to key competitors? An important tool in understanding your market position relative to that of competitors is to conduct a "SWOT" analysis. SWOT is an acronym for **S**trengths, **W**eaknesses, **O**pportunities, and **T**hreats. Strengths and weaknesses are about your company or the "internal environment." Opportunities and threats are about the market or "external environment."

Here are working definitions of each of the four concepts:

- Strengths: superior resources and skills that can be drawn on to exploit opportunities and deal with threats. Every business has strengths, beyond "product." Examples include product development capability, marketing capability, financial resources, management capability, information systems, and people.

- Weaknesses: deficiencies that inhibit the ability to perform or achieve results, and must be overcome to avoid failure. Every business also has weaknesses. Any of the items mentioned as possible strengths can be weaknesses if the item is holding the company back in some way.

- Opportunities: environmental trends with positive consequences. Opportunities may suggest a new basis for competitive advantage or present a possibility of improved performance (increased efficiency, sales, profits, or market share) if pursued. Examples include overall market growth, emerging customer segments, vulnerable competitors, political and cultural trends, technology trends, and economic trends.

- Threats: environmental trends with potentially negative impacts. Threats may impede implementation of strategy, increase risk, increase the people or cash resources required, or cause us to reduce expectations for business results. Threats are also called risks. The examples of opportunities mentioned above can also be threats if they have potentially negative consequences.

The music market is full of opportunities and threats that can have an impact on *all* competitors. Here's a key point: While each music business has a unique set of strengths and weaknesses, there are market opportunities and threats facing us all.

YOUR COMPETITIVE INTELLIGENCE SYSTEM

How do you secure information on competitors? Isn't it difficult to get accurate and useful data? Two key points here:

1. Virtually all information about the market and competitors is readily available.

2. The information is often free or inexpensive to gather.

So where does competitive intelligence come from? A detailed prescription is beyond the scope of this book, but here are some pointers to get you started.

Public Sources of Competitive and Market Information
The public sources listed below are generally free or inexpensive.

- Websites and collateral material of competitors
- Industry directories
- Trade publications
- Trade shows, events, and associations

- The general media
- Published research studies

Private Sources of Competitive and Market Information

Private sources of information allow you to screen out junk data by asking specific and detailed questions that are relevant to your competitive analysis. Be prepared to pay for information and service.

- Your network of personal contacts
- Third-party informants
- Internet search engines and research portals
- Market research firms and information brokers

YOUR COMPETITIVE DATABASE

Your competitive intelligence system may consist of a simple file folder with scribbled notes or a computerized database with detailed records on every direct and indirect competitor. Regardless of how you store the information, here are the basics to have at your disposal.

1. Basic profiles of leading direct competitors. In addition to name and contact information, the profile includes each competitor's product description, estimated sales volume, growth trend (up, down, or flat), and key strengths and weaknesses.

2. Estimated total market size and growth. It is important to see where you and your competitors fit in to the overall market. When you know the size of the total market and each competitor's estimated sales revenue, you can calculate market share.

3. Market trend information. Secure and organize information on economic, cultural, political, and technology trends that can have an impact on you and your competitors.

4. Source information. Create a list of places to go to get further information when you need it. Examples include publications, websites, or people in the know.

5. Sample materials. In the music industry it is relatively simple and inexpensive to secure recordings, promotional material, agency rosters, concert schedules, and publicity clippings on each of your key direct competitors. Keeping this on file not only keeps you in touch with their activities, but can also provide ideas for what to do or what to avoid in your own product and promotional strategies.

USING THE SEVEN LINKS

Now that you understand the seven links in the marketing chain, let's use them to develop even more detailed competitive profiles. Here's a shortcut to understanding your competitors: Write down the essence of their marketing plan.

Try this exercise. Fill in a few words about yourself and two more direct competitors in each row of the table below. This exercise can be sobering, motivating, and inspiring all at the same time. Note: This template is included in the Reference Section and on the CD-ROM.

Profile Element	You	Competitor One	Competitor Two
Product description	_____ _____ _____	_____ _____ _____	_____ _____ _____
Price range and strategy	_____ _____ _____	_____ _____ _____	_____ _____ _____
Promotional strategy	_____ _____ _____	_____ _____ _____	_____ _____ _____
Place/geographic territory	_____ _____ _____	_____ _____ _____	_____ _____ _____
Salesforce strategy	_____ _____ _____	_____ _____ _____	_____ _____ _____
Target customer	_____ _____ _____	_____ _____ _____	_____ _____ _____
Key strength	_____ _____ _____	_____ _____ _____	_____ _____ _____
Key weakness	_____ _____ _____	_____ _____ _____	_____ _____ _____

In Section Four ("Applying the Fundamentals in Your Music Business"), we'll begin putting the pieces of your business plan together.

KEY POINTS IN THIS CHAPTER

1. Competitors are other businesses or individuals who are going after the same target customer or buyer as you are.

2. Direct competitors are businesses that are similar to yours and in the same product category.

3. Indirect competitors are any products (goods or services) that go after the same target customer's attention and money, whether music/entertainment-oriented or not.

4. Direct competitors are generally easier to identify and understand than indirect competitors. As a result, indirect competitors are often perceived as mysterious.

5. To identify leading direct competitors, it is helpful to refer to your target customer profile. For example, one agent or promoter may target a substantially different set of customers from another, thus reducing the immediate competitive threat.

6. Every competitor (including you) has a unique set of **S**trengths, **W**eaknesses, **O**pportunities, and **T**hreats. Constructing a competitive "SWOT" analysis is a helpful tool in preparing competitive strategy.

7. Strengths and weaknesses are about an individual company. Opportunities and threats refer to overall market conditions that can have an effect—positive or negative—on all competitors.

8. Details about the market and about specific competitors are readily available. Your "competitive intelligence system" allows you to understand market conditions and how you and your competitors are dealing with them. Most market information is readily accessible and relatively inexpensive.

9. Public sources of information include websites, collateral material, the general media, published research studies, and trade publications, events, and associations. Private sources of information include your network of personal contacts, Internet search engines and research portals, and market research firms.

10. Your competitive database should include (a) basic profiles of leading direct competitors, (b) estimated total market size and growth, (c) market trend information, (d) source information, and (e) sample materials.

11. The dossier for each leading competitor includes information on product mix, price range and strategy, promotional strategy, place or geographic territory, salesforce strategy, target customer profile, key strengths, and key weaknesses.

APPLYING THE FUNDAMENTALS IN YOUR MUSIC BUSINESS

DOING THE NUMBERS—SETTING REALISTIC GOALS AND OBJECTIVES

Music people are often driven by creative or artistic goals and dreams and frequently downplay their financial and personal aspirations. Having realistic written goals and objectives is the best tool for managing the inherent challenges in balancing music, business, family, and other interests.

How much do I want to earn? How hard do I want to work? What am I willing to risk to get what I want? Many music people have never really addressed these questions. This chapter will provide a framework for setting realistic goals and objectives that are consistent with your values.

THE IMPORTANCE OF GOALS AND OBJECTIVES

There's an old expression that goes, "What gets measured, gets done." This is an important business truism. Having *written* business goals and objectives are essential for:

- Business planning
- Marketing and sales planning
- Creative development
- Personal development
- Congruity with personal values

You may be thinking, "I have goals in my head. I don't need to write them down." It's good that you have goals. It's better to write them down and turn them into a set of achievable objectives with milestones. That's what this chapter will show you how to do.

QUICK REVIEW: HOW ARE GOALS DIFFERENT FROM OBJECTIVES?

Here are those definitions again:

- Goal: a desired result, often long-term, and something good that you aspire to over a long period of time

- Objective: an aspect or subset of a goal that is specific, measurable, and achievable

For example, many people have a goal to get rich and retire young. That's a desirable result and likely to be a long-term proposition. As we did briefly in Chapter One, let's turn this goal into a set of objectives.

Objective: "Own a $2 million investment portfolio by age 60 and be able to live on the interest or dividends."

This is a clear statement of objectives. It is *specific* ($2 million in investments by age 60), *measurable* (can be tracked over time) and—for the sake of discussion—*achievable*.

Remember the definitions of strategy and tactics, also from Chapter One? Let's take a quick look one more time.

- Strategy: a decision made now that affects future activities. In other words, a strategy is a thought process leading to a decision and commitment, not necessarily the behavior or work itself.

- Tactic: an activity designed to achieve a desired result. Tactics are what you do to implement a strategy. Where strategy describes "what," tactics describe "how to."

In this context, goals relate to strategy; objectives relate to tactics. You need both. Since things change over time, it's important to keep a short-term and long-term perspective.

SETTING GOALS IN THREE CATEGORIES

Goals and objectives relate to all aspects of your music career and your personal life, not just finances. For most music people, goals fall neatly into three categories: creative, financial, and personal. Let's look at examples.

In each of the three categories below there is a list of possible goals. The part in quotes ("be a _____") is aimed at helping you articulate your goals for that subcategory. You do not necessarily need goals in all of these sample categories. In addition, you are likely to think of goal categories that are important to you and not listed here. Remember this is just a starting point.

Creative Goals

Creative or artistic goals are the long-term results that you desire, whether you make money from them or not. Goals in the creative category define the business playing field before adding the financial elements. Musical creativity is not limited to composition and performance. Agents, managers, and promoters also have creative goals. Examples of creative goals may include:

- Songs written, published, and recorded—"be a successful songwriter"
- Records produced and released—"be a successful recording artist"

- Airplay on radio, television, or online—"expose my music to the public via broadcast media"

- Show dates performed, booked, or promoted—"expose my music to the public via live events"

- Acts booked or managed—"represent the world's best acts and be a successful agent or manager"

- Award nominations and wins—"win a Grammy or other music industry award"

- Interviews, articles, and reviews published in the media—"be recognized in the media for excellence in the music industry"

- Endorsements and sponsorships—"earn a part of my income from promotional fees"

- Website visitors and fan club members—"have a network of loyal fans connected via the Internet"

- Participation in benefit shows or other pro bono work—"give a part of my time and talent back to charitable causes"

These are examples to get you thinking about your own creative goals. Let's move on to financial goals.

Financial Goals

Even if you are working in music part-time or on a not-for-profit basis, you need financial goals. Your financial goals need to tie to your creative goals. Once you do the numbers, you will get better grounded in reality. Your financial goals may include:

- Revenue from song royalties—"earn a living (or part thereof) as a published songwriter"

- Revenue from record royalties—"earn a living as a recording artist"

- Revenue from live performances—"earn a living as a stage performer or promoter"

- Revenue from commissions and fees—"earn a living as an agent or manager"

- Revenue from endorsements and sponsorships—"earn money from promotions"

- Revenue from merchandising or other sources—"have a catalog of merchandise that sustains the operation between tours or projects"

- Largest, smallest, and average target revenue by source—"build my reputation to command increasing prices, allowing me to be selective on projects"

- Profit (revenue minus expenses) —"be profitable and have something left over to save or invest"

- Return on investment (ROI) —"make a return on my cash and time investment that is as good or better than putting money into a savings account"

These examples should get you thinking about your financial goals. Let's continue with personal goals.

Personal Goals

Your creative and financial goals need to be consistent or in harmony with your personal goals. By identifying these goals up front, you can optimize all results and prevent problems down the road. Personal goals may include:

- How much you work in the course of a year—"work enough to make a living and get ahead while preventing burnout"

- How much vacation time, and what you do on vacation—"take a vacation that does not involve work"

- Family time, projects, and relationships—"have plenty of time for my family and personal life"

- Community involvement and activities—"contribute to or be involved with my community"

- Spiritual growth and activities—"have time to develop my spiritual beliefs" or "be active in my church"

- Educational development—"have time to learn new things, business and otherwise"

- Health maintenance—"stay youthful and live long"

- Exercise and fitness activities—"have time to stay fit"

- Hobbies and recreational activities—"have time to pursue my favorite leisure activities"

EXERCISE 1: YOUR THREE-YEAR GOALS

Where do you want to be in three years? Or looking at it another way, what do you need to do over the next three years to be satisfied with your progress? Write down the top three to five goals that come to mind in each of the three major categories. The idea is to articulate your primary goals so that you can turn them into objectives and milestones. You can refine this later using the template in the Reference Section and CD-ROM.

Creative Goals

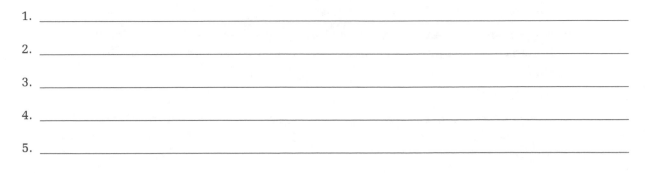

1. _____

2. _____

3. _____

4. _____

5. _____

Financial Goals

1. _____

2. _____

3. _____

4. _____

5. _____

Personal Goals

1. _____

2. _____

3. _____

4. _____

5. _____

TURNING GOALS INTO OBJECTIVES: WHEN IN DOUBT, QUANTIFY

When you feel those uneasy feelings coming on (like wondering if your goals are realistic), it's time to do the numbers. Quantifying your goals is the first step in designing a set of objectives that are specific, measurable, and achievable.

Everything—including nonfinancial goals—can be quantified in terms of number of units, pricing or revenue, expense budget, and timing or date the results are achieved. As they become quantified, your creative, financial, and personal goals turn into objectives. Here are a few examples of solid trackable objectives in each of the three categories:

Creative Objectives

- Write _____ new song (s) each month
- Release _____ new record (s) each year
- Perform, book, or promote _____ number of shows each year

Financial Objectives

- Earn $ _____ from publishing, recording, or performing each year
- Increase average performance fee or commission earned from $ _____ to $ _____ by _____ (date)
- Earn $ _____ from nontraditional sources (endorsements, merchandising) by _____ (date)

Personal Objectives

- Work _____ days per year (the rest is free time)
- Contribute $ _____ or _____ (time) to my local charity, church, school, or community
- Get my weight to _____ pounds and cholesterol level to _____

THREE KEY QUESTIONS ABOUT SETTING OBJECTIVES

Like your goals, your objectives are unique to you. While circumstances may dictate what is feasible to a degree, you generally have control over your objectives. To that end, here are three key questions to ask yourself as you turn your goals into objectives.

1. How much do I want to earn?

2. How hard do I want to work?

3. How much am I willing to sacrifice?

The answers will help keep you focused. They also serve as checks and balances. For example, if you want to make a lot of money but not work very hard, you'll need to determine if that is feasible. Likewise, the "risk vs. reward" concept discussed in Chapter Two comes into play. If you are too risk-averse, it may limit your earning capability. There are no right or wrong answers here—just use the three questions to guide your thinking.

WHAT'S ACTUALLY ACHIEVABLE?

How much can I possibly earn in music? Do I need to aspire to stardom to make it all worthwhile? Most music people want to at least be able to pay for their habits. Others want to make a modest living doing music full-time. Others want to get rich and retire young. Theoretically, all of the above are possible. Your business plan—including goals and objectives—is your single most important tool for achieving what you want and staying in control throughout the process.

THE SCHOOLTEACHER PARADIGM

Let's set the media-induced get-rich-quick schemes to the side for a moment. Consider the example of a typical public schoolteacher in North America. Good teachers have creative skills and goals. They are respected in the community and often viewed as underpaid and underappreciated. Sound familiar? Let's compare the characteristics of a schoolteacher to those of a music person and see where it takes us. By the way, the comparison can be made easily for performers, songwriters, agents, managers, and promoters alike.

Item	Schoolteacher	Music Person
College education	Required	Not required
Certification or license	Required	Occasionally required
Preparation for the job	Lesson plans, materials	Songs, rehearsal, planning
Communication skill	Required	Required
Deal with tough crowds	Occasionally	Occasionally
Term of contract	Minimum one year	Minimum one performance
Health plan, other benefits	Full coverage	Infrequently
Retirement plan	Teacher's pension	Social Security maybe
Pay scale	$20K–$50K per year	Varies widely
Vacation	Two months with pay	As long as you want, unpaid

Here's the point: It is entirely fair and realistic to work toward schoolteachers' wages and benefits as a basic model for modest business success in the music industry. While many music people aspire to or are already making more, too many music people settle for less!

As you set your financial objectives, keep the following in mind:

- There are geographical variations across North America in terms of prevailing wage standards and cost of living. Adjust your objectives to your location.

- After accounting for all the time put in on the job, many music people make less than the federal minimum wage. This ties to the "how hard do I want to work?" question.

• Regardless of what you are making *now* through music, plan to increase or at least control how much you make relative to your time and cash investment. Pay attention to inflation and changing family needs as well as your long-term goals in the three categories above.

HOW TO FORECAST SALES REVENUE

Sales don't just happen by accident. You need a revenue plan—a set of financial objectives—that is specific, measurable, and achievable. Here is a simple formula for forecasting revenue:

Total $ revenue = units sold x average $ revenue per unit

Units and revenue per unit are calculated differently depending on your role in the music industry. Detailed forecast methodology for all types of music businesses is beyond the scope of this book. However, the basic principles illustrated here apply to your planning process whether you are already doing budgeting and forecasting or not. Here's a quick reference table to define what we mean by "units."

Industry Role	Unit of Measure	Basis for Average $ Revenue per Unit
Performer	Live show dates performed	Average performance fee per date
Songwriter	Airplay or record sales for each song in catalog	Royalty rate per performance or record sold
Agent	Show dates booked for each artist	Average commission $ per date booked
Manager	Represented artists	Average commission $ based on artist's total earnings (performance fees, royalties, merchandising, etc.)
Promoter	Show dates or events presented	Average ticket sales per show (ticket price x paid attendance)

Here's a sample forecast template. Let's use a four-piece band as an example:

Item	Last Year	This Year	Next Year	Year 2	Year 3
Number of show dates	24	36	60	90	120
Average price per date	$400	$ 600	$750	$1,200	$2,000
Total performance revenue	$9,600	$ 21,600	$45,000	$108,000	$240,000
Expenses @ 50% of revenue	$4,800	$ 10,800	$22,500	$54,000	$120,000
Gross profit margin	$4,800	$ 10,800	$22,500	$54,000	$120,000
Number of band members	4	4	4	4	4
Average $ per member	$1,200	$2,700	$5,625	$13,500	$30,000
Target $ per member	$1,200	$2,500	$5,000	$12,000	$25,000
Variance $ per member	$ –	$200	$625	$1,500	$5,000

This quick forecast is not a full-blown budget, which would be beyond the scope of this book. Still, you can estimate business expenses (50% of gross revenue is a good rule of thumb) and calculate how much revenue is left over per person. This is the money that you have to live on, or contribute to your personal budget.

EXERCISE 2: YOUR THREE-YEAR OBJECTIVES

Using the above format, let's plan one key financial objective for you or your company over a three-year period. Choose a category of objective that has real revenue potential for you—your "bread and butter."

It's a good idea to always look at a five-year window: one year back, the current year, plus three more years. Last year and this year are reference points that help you get started. If you are just now entering the business world, leave the "last year" column blank.

Item	Last Year	This Year	Next Year	Year 2	Year 3
What:					
Number of units					
Average $ per unit					
Total $ revenue					

This exercise is designed to get you thinking three years in advance. It also helps you understand the variables (like units and pricing) and the extent to which you can or cannot control them.

THE LURE OF THE ENTERTAINMENT INDUSTRY—ARE MY GOALS REALISTIC?

If your music business information comes primarily from the general media—television, radio, newspapers, and magazines—you would conclude that all music people are either rich or dead. That's a bit of an exaggeration. Still, think about it. Working music people are rarely talked about in the media. This is especially true of agents, managers, promoters, and other behind-the-scenes music people.

Some people are lured to the music field by the promise of "sex, drugs, and rock 'n' roll" along with the American Dream scenario of getting rich doing something glamorous. I trust that most readers understand that the chances of getting rich quick in music are about the same as in any other business category: pretty low.

Is there a middle ground between celebrity and oblivion? You bet. In fact, that's where most of the million or so music people in North America are: somewhere in between. Here's the point. You don't need to be a superstar to make a good living in music. Be careful as you observe or emulate the portrayals of music celebrities in the media. They can be illustrative and entertaining, but seldom serve as a real business model.

SHARING YOUR GOALS WITH OTHERS

Who do I share my goals and objectives with? Who needs to know and at what level of detail? There are three basic types of relationships to consider in addressing these questions.

1. Family and friends. You are likely to be most comfortable sharing goal information with those who know you best and are close to you. While they may not be interested in the short-term objectives and the fine details, they are generally interested in understanding where you are headed long-term from a creative, financial, and personal standpoint.

2. Business associates. Your business partners, investors, and key creditors are especially interested in your financial goals and objectives. While less concerned with creative and personal issues, they are likely to care about understanding how the financial pieces of your business fit together. Your business plan (or elements of it) becomes the medium for sharing the information.

3. Your support team. Staff, service vendors (like publicists, arrangers, and recording engineers), and co-workers need to know where you are headed. For example, if you are a performer working with an agent or manager, it is important for you to share detailed goals and objectives and monitor progress together actively.

A WORD OF CAUTION

Your competitors would love to know all about your plans for success, just as much as you would like to know theirs. Be careful how much information you share with whom. Long-term goals like being a successful performer and songwriter are benign enough, but details on how you plan to achieve goals are proprietary or confidential. In other words, tell family, friends, business associates, and support team just enough to satisfy their needs. That's where the expression "need-to-know basis" comes from.

KEY POINTS IN THIS CHAPTER

1. Goals and objectives are essential for business planning, marketing and sales planning, creative development, and personal development.

2. Writing down goals and objectives is a powerful exercise that provides clarity and the ability to communicate the information with others. "What gets measured, gets done."

3. A goal is a desired result that is often long-term. An objective is an aspect or subset of a goal which is specific, measurable, and achievable.

4. Goals drive the strategy. Objectives drive the tactical operating plan.

5. Goals can be organized into three categories: creative, financial, and personal. Congruity among all three types of goals is important in business.

6. Once you have written goals in the three categories, they can be turned into a set of objectives. Both financial and nonfinancial goals can be quantified in terms of number of units, pricing or revenue, expense budgets, and date the results are achieved.

7. You have control over your objectives as long as you keep them realistic. Ask yourself three important questions: (1) How much do I want to earn?, (2) How hard do I want to work?, and (3) How much am I willing to sacrifice or risk to achieve my objectives?

8. The range of objectives in the music industry—like any other business—is wide. Some music people want to make a living in music, others just want to work part-time. Still others aspire to get rich and retire young. We all need well-defined goals and objectives to remain grounded in reality.

9. Your sales forecast flows from financial and creative objectives. The formula for forecasting sales is: Total $ revenue = units sold x average $ revenue per unit.

10. When creating a sales forecast, start by recognizing actual sales results for last year and this year, then plan three years into the future. This is called the "Five-Year Window."

11. The media portrays music business celebrities as rich and famous. In reality, a relatively high percentage of music people work part-time and/or make a modest living from their music business pursuits. Beware of the influence of media stereotypes as you set your goals and objectives.

12. Beware of revealing private goals and strategy to your competitors. Share your goals and objectives with your friends and family, business associates, and support team on a selective or "need-to-know basis."

CHAPTER SEVENTEEN

COMMON SENSE BUSINESS LESSONS FOR THE UNCOMMON MUSIC WORLD

In my consulting work, I often get questions like, "That planning stuff all sounds good, but where are the shortcuts? How can I get rich and retire young without having to do all that stuff?" My answer is that there are no gimmicks or secrets in the world of business. Planning is the best "shortcut," and it is a lot less costly than the trial-and-error alternatives.

In this chapter, we'll look at six common sense business lessons that will help you optimize your planning along with the other fundamentals of business. See if you can relate to any of the "common pitfall" examples cited throughout the lessons.

LESSON 1: WHEN IN DOUBT, QUANTIFY

I present this lesson first because it is probably the one you will use most frequently. Ever wonder if your goals or objectives are realistic? Have a knotty problem to solve? Wonder where the money is going to come from? We've all felt uneasy about things like this. The first thing to do when you feel anxious is to pinch yourself, remember this lesson, and take a look at the numbers.

Common Pitfalls

Here are examples of danger signals that lead to business problems:

- Having no budget or financial tracking. You'll never know how you are doing if you don't keep track. For some music people this is obvious, for others a revelation.

- Not understanding how long things take or how much things cost. How many hours do you spend in rehearsal or traveling to gigs? What's your hourly rate when you factor everything in?

- Making decisions based on gut feelings, intuition, or how others have done things. Intuition is very important, but it is helpful to apply reason to decisions involving money and time commitments.

Recommended Action

Most music is logical, systematic, and mathematical, which makes it less of a stretch for music people to "do the numbers" than for other creative types. Use this to your advantage. Start with a basic revenue and expense forecast for any project before going to work. Think of your budget as an "original composition," something that you create and have control over. When thinking through your three-year goals and objectives, see what expenses are feasible in the first year, regardless of where you want to be in year three. Do the math and let the numbers guide you.

> *Some music people—especially performers or songwriters—may say, "I'm the creative force in my business. I have someone else to deal with the money."*

While that may be true, there will be times when you are called upon to make decisions that involve time and money. In anticipation of that, remember the lesson: "When in doubt, quantify."

LESSON 2: THE CHAIN IS ONLY AS STRONG AS THE WEAKEST LINK

Remember this age-old expression? We hear it all the time. We've already begun to apply it to your music business. Chapters Nine through Fifteen discussed the seven links in the marketing chain. We've already made the point that each of the seven links is important, and if one link is weak or missing, it compromises all results. Here are some more examples:

Common Pitfalls

- Thinking that the music is all that matters or that a strong stage show or record can make up for weaknesses in other areas. For example, as a promoter, you could have the best acts in the world booked in a great venue, but if no one knows about the show or if tickets are priced out of the market, it doesn't matter from a business perspective. Each link needs to be strong.

- Focusing on one area of the business to the exclusion of the others. This goes beyond the marketing plan. Your business—even a one-person company—has five functional areas: (1) marketing and sales, (2) finance and accounting, (3) product development, (4) production and operations including information systems, and (5) general management. Weakness in any of these areas jeopardizes overall results.

Recommended Action

Go for balanced strength in each of the key areas of the business. The first step is one that you have already taken: being aware of what it takes to run a business. You now know that a business has five functional areas and the marketing chain has seven links. If you pay attention to each of those elements, you can be confident that you are covering the bases.

LESSON 3: THE BUSINESS STUFF—ESPECIALLY SALES—IS A FULL-TIME JOB

If you already operate a music business, you know how true the above statement is. When was the last time you worked a 40-hour week? Even if you work for someone else, you know that operating a music business is demanding and time-consuming.

Many music people work day jobs and pursue their musical business interests on a part-time basis. This is fine if your goals and objectives are consistent with practical realities. At a certain point you will *need* to quit your day job in order to focus full-time on the music business. Additionally, you will need to hire or contract with additional people as the business grows.

Focus, expertise, and image with customers all come into play here. While it is tempting to let someone else handle the business, you need to understand the risks.

Common Pitfalls

- Hiring friends or relatives, even on a part-time basis. There's nothing inherently wrong with this, but the risk is one that is common to the music business. Remember the band story in our overview? It's so common for performers to have a spouse, relative, or friend do booking, bookkeeping, or other support functions, only to find out that the person lacks the skill or time to make a long-term difference.

- Assuming that all business people are selfish crooks. Some music people think that agents, managers, and promoters are only in it for the money, or are "rip-off artists." Every business—music and otherwise—has its share of opportunists and criminals. The media reminds us of those in the music and entertainment industry because of its glamour. However, there are plenty of reputable and qualified music business people with integrity.

Recommended Action

Recognize immediately that no one person has all the skills and time needed to build a music business. If you try to do everything yourself, you may succeed to a point and then find that you can't grow—creatively, financially, or personally—beyond that point. Build your team with people who are well qualified in their respective areas.

LESSON 4: BUILD ON STRENGTHS AND DELEGATE THE WEAKNESSES

Remember the concept of the "SWOT" analysis in Chapter Fifteen? It is important and helpful to identify your company's strengths and weaknesses. Once you understand them, what do you do next? For many people, the natural inclination is to go to work on the weaknesses.

For example, let's say you are a manager with strengths in negotiation and artist relations, but weaknesses in the areas of accounting and finance. One approach is to drop what you are doing and learn accounting and finance. Go to night school, buy computer software, practice in your spare time, and hope you get it right. After six months, you are likely to have marginally improved in finance. In the meantime, your other work may have suffered. It's also possible that your self-esteem may be dampened as you struggle with the new material.

Delegation is generally a better alternative. Focus on what you do best and have other people do the same. If you are weak in finance or other aspects of your business, find an expert to pick up the slack rather than trying to become an expert in a new area yourself.

Common Pitfalls

- Failing to identify strengths and weaknesses objectively. This works both ways. Some people exaggerate their strengths, and others exaggerate their weaknesses. You may need an outside perspective from customers, staff, friends, or family in order to get a clear picture.

- Setting unrealistic expectations on how long it takes to learn special skills. Whatever you are good at now probably comes easily to you. Can you learn sales negotiation as easily as you learned songwriting? Will it take as long to create a marketing plan as it does to secure a record deal? Understand that new things take longer than you might imagine.

Recommended Action

First, beware of isolated self-assessment. Do your SWOT analysis with input from your team, friends, or family as a reality check. Then, work at what you are good at and like doing and hire out the rest. Remember that virtually any task—from vehicle maintenance to promotion—can be delegated to someone outside of your organization. While you'll have to pay for professional services, you are likely to save time and money both now and in the long run. You don't have time to learn brand-new skills quickly enough to make a difference in the fast-paced business world—unless it's a hobby or labor of love.

Consider the example of the self-represented performer or songwriter. Should you do all your own bookings and negotiate recording and publishing deals on your own, or engage an agent, manager, or lawyer to represent you? The answer flows from your specific goals and objectives as discussed in Chapter Sixteen. It's a matter of planning and timing more than cost.

LESSON 5: UNDERSTAND YOUR CUSTOMERS AND GIVE THEM WHAT THEY WANT, PLUS A LITTLE MORE.

Your customers have needs and expectations. They will evaluate your performance (musical or business) based on a set of criteria. As you do the customer profiling exercise discussed in Chapter Fourteen, you develop an increased understanding of the buying criteria.

There is both a risk and an opportunity here. If you fail to deliver what your customers want, they may not come back for more. Adding to the risk, they may not tell *you* what went wrong, but they are likely to tell others (like prospective customers, competitors, or the press). If you deliver slightly above their expectations, they are more likely to want more, and also more likely to tell others about you.

Common Pitfalls

- Lacking definition of target customer profiles. If you don't understand your customers, you will never know if you are meeting their needs.

- Assuming that "if we do it, they will buy it." For example, experienced promoters know that simply booking name acts is not enough. The venue, date, promotion, pricing, and logistics (like audience parking or transportation access) all need to be consistently good in order to please the crowd and keep them coming back for more.

- Cutting corners on promotion materials to save money. Being "penny-wise and pound-foolish" generally does more harm than good. Conversely, consistent quality makes a good impression and often comes as a pleasant surprise to your customers.

Recommended Action

First, establish a clear definition of your market and focus your efforts on those customers. Don't worry about a mass market because there isn't one. Your target customers have needs and buying criteria that are unique to them, but they can be identified up front. Exceed your customers' expectations for quality and consistency in whatever you do.

LESSON 6: UNDERSTAND YOUR COMPETITORS AND DIFFERENTIATE YOURSELF FROM THEM

If you are *exactly* like your competitors, lowest price or closest personal relationship becomes the ultimate purchase criterion. Is your act just like all the rest? Do your songs sound just like those of _____ (fill in famous songwriter's name here)? As an agent or manager, are your acts just like your competitors'? Do you handle those acts in any special ways? As a promoter, are you offering shows that provide excellent entertainment value when compared to sports, movies, or theater?

In Chapter Fifteen, we discussed how to identify and understand your competition. The point here is that to be better, you need to be different. Being different for its own sake does not necessarily mean that you are better, but you can't be better by being the same.

Common Pitfalls

- Assuming that we need to be just like our competitors in order to succeed. This is an error in logic. It's fine to learn from competitors and develop comparable strengths, but copying can lead to problems.

- Ignoring competition, especially the indirect kind. "We have no competition." Think again. Remember all those examples of direct and indirect competition? Whether you are looking for show dates to play, artists to record your songs, acts to represent, venues to buy your acts, or the public to buy concert tickets, someone else is going after your customers' time and money.

Recommended Action

The first step is to conduct your competitive analysis. Identify the top five competitors in each relevant category, including their strengths and weaknesses. List the similarities and differences between you and your competition, and focus on promoting the positive differences in your marketing plan. Remember that you need to be as good as the competition before you can be better—but that does not mean copying or promoting the similarities.

Do the six lessons above sound like common sense? Hopefully the answer is "yes." The idea here is to reinforce what you already know so you can apply it to your music business with confidence.

KEY POINTS IN THIS CHAPTER

1. The only secret to success in business is that there are no secrets. Business principles apply to the music industry just as they do to other fields.

2. There are no gimmicks or get-rich-quick schemes in modern business. Apply common sense to what you know rather than look for shortcuts.

3. Lesson 1: "When in doubt, quantify." Understand how much things cost and how long things take to accomplish. "Do the numbers."

4. Lesson 2: "The chain is only as strong as the weakest link." Strengthen your business with balance in each of the five functional areas: marketing and sales, finance and accounting, product development, production and operations (including information systems), and general management.

5. Lesson 3: "The business stuff—especially sales—is a full-time job." No one person has all the skills and time needed to build a music business. Build your team with people who are well-qualified in their respective areas.

6. Lesson 4: "Build on strengths and delegate the weaknesses." Do your "SWOT" analysis with input from your team, friends, or family as a reality check. Then, work at what you are good at and like doing, and hire out the rest.

7. Lesson 5: "Understand your customers and give them what they want, plus a little more." Establish a clear definition of your market, focus your efforts on those customers, and exceed their expectations.

8. Lesson 6: "Understand your competitors and differentiate yourself from them." Identify your leading competitors, including their strengths and weaknesses. List the similarities and differences between you and your competition, and focus on promoting the positive differences in your marketing plan.

CHAPTER EIGHTEEN

PUTTING IT ALL TOGETHER

f you've gotten this far, you have been exposed to most of the pieces of a business plan, except the budgets and financial schedules. Here's what we've covered so far:

SECTION ONE: THE ART OF MAKING GOOD DECISIONS

- Mission and motivation: understanding why you are in the music business
- Preliminary planning: understanding what's involved in starting a new business
- Market overview: understanding the scope and structure of the music industry
- Risk analysis: deciding when to quit your day job

SECTION TWO: CREATING YOUR ESSENTIAL BUSINESS PLAN

- Rationale: eight reasons to have a business plan
- Contents: five "chapters" of your business plan and their relative importance
- Planning flow: from mission statement to daily action list

SECTION THREE: BUILDING YOUR BRAND

- Marketing vs. sales: understanding key functions of the two related disciplines
- The seven links in the marketing chain: (1) product strategy, (2) pricing strategy, (3) promotional strategy, (4) sales channel strategy, (5) salesforce strategy, (6) customer profiles, and (7) competitive environment

SECTION FOUR: APPLYING THE FUNDAMENTALS IN YOUR MUSIC BUSINESS

- Goals and objectives: realistic milestones on the road to success
- Common sense: six lessons from the business world applied to music

So where are you now in terms of your planning process? If you have not done so already, this is a good time to start putting the ideas and material for your business plan together. This applies to you whether you are:

- In business already but don't have a written plan
- In business and have a partial plan
- In business, have a plan, and are contemplating growth or the launch of new products
- Not in business yet, but thinking about it

YOUR BUSINESS PLANNING CHECKLIST

In Chapter Seven we identified the five primary elements or stages of the planning process:

- Plan Element 1: The Mission Statement
- Plan Element 2: The Brand Positioning Statement
- Plan Element 3: The Three-Year Product Plan
- Plan Element 4: The Operating Plan
- Plan Element 5: The Daily Action List

What else do you need? Here are the additional elements:

- Operational strategy. Creating the product is important, but delivering it consistently and profitably points to your business's operations and its ability to execute the plan. This ties to Plan Element 4 and the financial schedules. Operational elements include:

—Location and infrastructure: workspace, computer systems, vehicles, equipment, telecommunications

—Licenses and business registrations: any required state, local, or federal authorization to conduct business; corporation documents if applicable

—Staff organization and benefits: payroll, insurance, employee policies and evaluation procedures, reporting structure

—Marketing plan: tactical implementation plan (specific methods and costs) for the strategies discussed in Section Three ("Building Your Brand") of this book

—Accounting and success measurement: management, financial, and tax reporting policies and procedures

- Financial schedules. The forecasting exercise in Chapter Sixteen got you thinking about revenue three years into the future. In addition to your revenue plan, your business plan includes expense budgets and income statements (also called profit and loss or "P&L" statements). Note: While detailed discussion of how to do budgeting is beyond the scope of this book, we have included simplified financials in the Reference Section and on the CD-ROM.
- Sources of working capital. When you start or develop a business, there is seldom enough revenue from basic sales operations to cover initial expenses

and the costs involved in growth. Many businesses fail because they cannot cover expenses in the early days. Identify in advance where your working capital will come from.

Note: The items above are presented in checklist form in the Reference Section and on the CD-ROM.

WHERE CAN I GET THE CASH I NEED TO BUILD MY BUSINESS?

Your cash needs also change over time. Understanding your future cash flow is another benefit of planning three years ahead rather than one year or not at all. "Where will I get the money?" The answer depends largely on how much you need. Your business plan will point you in the right direction. For review, see the section in Chapter Four about viable and nonviable sources of working capital.

FREQUENTLY ASKED QUESTIONS ABOUT BUSINESS PLANS

Here are the answers to common questions about the process of constructing a business plan.

1. Who's going to read the plan? First and foremost, it's for you and your staff. Both the strategy and the operating details are foundations for your business. If you are a one-person business, it is still essential to write things down and keep the details organized. If you have investors or are seeking financing, remember that those people will need to review and understand the plan. In most cases, stakeholders like investors or financiers will require the plan before they will advance funds.

2. How long and detailed should the document be? There is no single standard for length of a business plan. It depends on the complexity of the business, how much preparation or homework you've done, and your personal style. That said, most people won't read a long document, even if they have a financial stake in the business. They want the essence, the highlights, the bullets, the executive version. To that end, the best plans have four primary sections:

Section 1: Strategic overview. This section includes the five "chapters" as described in Chapter Six. Keep this to 10–15 pages of text.

Section 2: Tactical marketing plan. This section covers the seven links in the marketing chain, spelled out for the next 24 months. Keep this to 6–10 pages of text.

Section 3: Financial schedules. The essence of the financials and key metrics have already been presented in the strategic overview. The financial section includes detailed summaries in spreadsheet form, by account by month, for the next 12 months of the fiscal year, plus annual summaries for the following two years. The pages of the financial section include (a) revenue plan, (b) expense budget, (c) cash flow analysis (including sources of cash in addition to normal business operations), (d) income statement or P&L, (e) capital expense budget, and (f) balance sheet. See the Reference Section and CD-ROM for samples of this format.

Section 4: Appendix or Reference Section. This is the place to put sample promotion materials, market statistics, publicity reprints, detailed competitive analysis, job descriptions, employee policies, or any other items that you want to have organized and in the same place as the rest of the plan. Keep your audience in mind: financial people like to see market statistics and trend information; employees like to see vacation policies and insurance benefit program details.

Estimated pages	One-product business	Multi-product Business
Strategic Overview	10	15
Tactical Marketing	6	10
Financials	6	6
Reference	5	50
Total Pages	**27**	**31**

Final result: The main document is 20–30 pages of text, 6 pages of financials and the appendix items, which could range from 5–50 pages of additional material.

3. What about an executive summary? Do I need one? How long should it be? A true executive summary is a one- or two-page document that includes the essence of the whole business plan. It is helpful when seeking financing, especially when many people are reviewing the plan. Executive summaries are generally not necessary for internal staff or your own use.

4. What format is best? How about a ring binder? Ring binders are fine, but I suggest the coil or spiral binding that you can get at copy shops. Why? Two reasons. First, a ring binder is clunky and hard to use unless you spread it out on a big desk or table (which makes it hard for your rich uncle to read on an airplane). Also, contents of ring binders mysteriously disappear or get rearranged. A more subjective reason involves the initial impression of the document. A bound book simply looks better and sends the message that you are committed and have done your homework. By the way, the production costs for the two formats are about the same.

5. How often should I update the plan? Annually, with semi-annual adjustments to the revenue plan and expense budgets. While mission statements and multi-year product plans change very little, the operating plan needs to be updated regularly. The idea is to do a revised three-year plan every year. Remember the "five-year window"—how we looked at one year back, the current year, plus three years? If you do that every year, you are revising an existing plan rather than starting from scratch each time. Each year, one year of history drops off and a new year is added on. As you revise, you'll notice your original thought process. This allows you to monitor your own progress and accuracy in forecasting as time goes on.

6. How long does it take to write a business plan like this one? The range is big here, depending on how much preparation you've already done and how comfortable or experienced you are with writing. Once you have thought through the strategic issues, writing the plan down and running numbers can take anywhere from 20–60 hours, spread out over a two- to four-week period. The first one will take longer than the next annual revision. I also suggest working on the plan steadily for a few weeks rather than sporadically for several months.

Does 20–60 hours seem like a long or short time to you? Consider how long it takes to develop your performing act, write great songs, create a roster of top talent, or prepare a major concert or festival. Doesn't your business idea deserve a few extra days' work in order to prevent problems and optimize your chances of success?

KEY POINTS IN THIS CHAPTER

1. The planning process applies to new or existing music businesses alike. You can apply the principles whether you are already in business or just thinking about it.

2. Your business planning checklist includes elements from each section in this book and from the five "chapters" of a business plan described in Chapter Six. Before writing the plan, pull all the elements—your notes, figures, and other materials—together in one place.

3. Operational strategy includes details covering (1) location and infrastructure, (2) licenses and business registrations, (3) staff organization and benefits, (4) marketing plan, and (5) accounting and success measurement.

4. Most music businesses need operating capital—cash to pay the bills—that does not come from day-to-day sales revenue. There are viable and nonviable sources of cash.

5. The audience for your business plan starts with yourself, and includes staff and stakeholders like investors or financiers. Write the plan with the assumption that it will be shared, even if you are currently a one-person business.

6. Concise business plans include four sections: strategic overview, tactical marketing plan, financial schedules, and appendix or Reference Section. The grand total ranges from about 25–80 pages, depending on the complexity of the business and your style.

7. Coil or spiral binding is a better presentation than a ring binder. The production costs for the two formats are about the same.

8. Revise the operating plan including the financials once every year so you're always looking at a "five-year window"—one year back, the current year, and three years into the future.

9. Once you have thought through the strategic issues and done the other basic preparation, the actual writing of a business plan takes 20–60 hours spread over 2–4 weeks.

10. You and your business deserve the effort that it takes to put the plan together.

11. "If it's not written down, it's not a plan." As we've said throughout, the details need to be captured in writing so they can be shared with others. The writing process is also a clarifying and creative experience.

CHAPTER NINETEEN

WORDS OF ENCOURAGEMENT— MORE COMMON SENSE LESSONS

For some of you, this chapter may reinforce things you already know. For others, it may be the most important part of the book. It contains five more common sense lessons from the big world of business, all of which are relevant and applicable to any music business or music person.

LESSON 1: PLANNING IS YOUR FIRST AND BEST BUSINESS INVESTMENT

Have you heard the expression, "Ready, fire, aim"? It is usually used to describe people who jump into a project without knowing what they are doing. Throughout this book, we've discussed how to plan and the benefits of writing down your plans. What happens if you don't? The big risk is that you may waste time and money—yours and others'—as you pursue the wrong business path.

Common Pitfalls

Leaping ahead without the benefit of market knowledge. How can you make strategic marketing decisions without understanding the market? You can't. "But I don't know how much to charge, let alone how to promote myself, so I'll just take whatever they are offering." This is how music people get exploited by the unscrupulous criminals that (unfortunately) do get into the business.

Asking for investment capital without knowing how much you need, where it will be spent, or how it will be paid back. "I know a rich guy who likes my music—I'll ask him to be my backer." Any investor who is worth working with long-term will ask what you are going to do with the money and how you are going to provide a return on the investment. Sure, parents and friends may kick in some gas or rent money once in a while, but that is not enough to build and sustain a music business.

Making decisions on gut feelings or by copying others' mistakes. "I just know this will work. It's the same thing that _____ (your friend or an admired colleague) did." First, go back to lesson one in Chapter Seventeen: "When in doubt, quantify." You may not think you are in doubt, but did you run your numbers? Further, the person or business you admire *may not be as successful as you think they are*, besides the fact that their situation is different from yours.

Recommended Action

This book is all about planning and taking conscious steps to move your music business in a positive direction. Follow the template provided here: define the business, understand the market, and analyze the risk—as outlined in Section One ("The Art of Making Good Decision"). Then go on to constructing your business plan and marketing strategy as discussed in Sections Two and Three.

LESSON 2: NO PRODUCT SELLS ITSELF

Can you relate to any of the following?

- "We'll play a lot of shows and build our fan base, then record and get rich."

- "I'll get my songs recorded by big acts. All I need is one hit in order to make a fortune."

- "Our roster of acts is so strong, we'll have to turn down gigs."

- "Everything lines up for this show—great acts, a great venue, and no competition. We'll sell out immediately."

I've heard versions of these scenarios many times. They are all making the assumption that the product sells itself. That's a faulty assumption.

Common Pitfalls

Assuming "if we provide it, they will buy it." You can't bank on sales based solely on your reputation or the strength of a product that you and a few others believe in. This leaves you vulnerable to both direct and indirect competitors.

Assuming that buyers will pick up the phone and call you. Anyone who's worked the phones knows that customers are hard to reach and even harder to get a response from. Relying only on incoming inquiries is a potential mistake.

Failing to follow-through on sales contacts and operational details (contracting, paperwork, promotion, etc.). The follow-up is your responsibility. Sure, there are a few very professional and personable customers who will pick up the slack if you don't. But there aren't enough of them out there to build and sustain your business. The good ones get tired of doing your work for you, and will ultimately move on.

Recommended Action

Be sure that the sales function of your business is covered by someone who likes to sell, knows how to sell, and is properly compensated. This ties to the profile of your salesforce as described in Chapter Thirteen.

LESSON 3: ARTISTIC INTEGRITY AND COMMERCIAL VIABILITY ARE INTRINSICALLY COMPATIBLE

I coined this phrase several years ago while sitting through a tedious panel discussion at a music trade show. At issue was the future growth and development of an entire genre of music. People in the discussion were concerned that (and I'm virtually quoting here) "if we get too successful the music will suffer." For many music people, the idea of "suffering for the music" is so ingrained that achieving commercial or financial success is almost incomprehensible. To do so would require "selling out"—compromising artistic integrity for the sake of money.

What? One more time? Run that by me again? Where does it say that music people have to work three part-time, nonmusic jobs to pay the expenses for the "privilege" to play low-paying gigs *so the music will sound better*? This entire book is about getting over those feelings and moving on. You can have *both* musical and financial success. They are not mutually exclusive.

Common Pitfalls

- Believing that the rules of business do not apply to the music industry. "Music business? That's an oxymoron. You can't apply common sense to music. I'll never be successful, but I love doing it."

- Assuming that business is evil and that music overcomes evil through its art. "All agents, managers, record labels, and lawyers are crooks. I got burned once, so they must all be out to get us."

- Believing that for the music to sound good, the musicians must be "starving artists." This ties to the "suffer for the music" scenario described above.

Recommended Action

First, simply observe that many successful people in the music business lead positive lives and create great art without compromising one for the other. You can certainly recognize the work of music industry people who have become role models for both peers and children, as well as major contributors to social, political, and religious causes.

LESSON 4: THE BIGGEST MARKETING CHALLENGE IS STANDING OUT FROM THE COMPETITION

Whether you are a performer, songwriter, agent, manager, or promoter, you have lots of competitors. We discussed the competitive environment in detail in Chapter Fifteen. Why bring it up again now? Because many music people seem to forget that their customers have too many positive choices. If all of those choices blur together, the customer is likely to succumb to the lure of the indirect competitors who have more resources.

Common Pitfalls

Assuming that fans and colleagues hear about your act, song, record, or show by mental telepathy. "We made a record but it didn't go anywhere. I still have 950 of them in boxes in my garage." How was it promoted and distributed? Did you tell anyone other than your family and friends that it was available?

Forgetting about indirect competition. Here we go again. The sports, film, and game industries want our fans—music fans—to spend time and money with them. What are you doing to rise above their din?

Assuming that people have an infinite supply of time, let alone money. "It's been three weeks and they haven't returned my call. It must be because they don't care." Not necessarily. How much discretionary time do *you* have? Put yourself in the position of a promoter, record label, or manager who is bombarded with information from acts and songwriters that want gigs. They can't get to all of them. That's why some companies return unsolicited materials—unopened. It's not about you, it's about time and attention.

Recommended Action

First, focus on customers who are targetable vs. the "mass market." This ties to the customer profiling techniques discussed in Chapter Fourteen. Once you've identified your target customers, promote positive differentiation of your product to set yourself apart from the pack. While there are no guarantees, you will increase your chances of rising above the "noise level" and getting closer to your objectives. Also, understanding and mastering time management is essential for success in the music business. By respecting your own and others' time, you will develop ways to make it easy for people to decide to buy what you are selling.

LESSON 5: IT'S OK TO BE RISK-AVERSE.

Throughout this book, we've talked about both the risks and the opportunities inherent in the music industry. Let's be clear: the concept of risk applies to any business, music or otherwise. Some people thrive on risk; others tolerate and manage it; still others just can't handle it. As we discussed in Chapter Four, you can enjoy a successful career in music regardless of your tolerance for risk. Simply put, it's OK to be risk-averse.

Common Pitfalls

Leaping into business without assessing your feelings about risk. "I just had to do it. I couldn't wait any longer. After I spent my life savings on producing the CD, I freaked out. Now I'm applying for jobs in other fields. At least I'll get benefits and a steady paycheck."

Assuming that the only way to be involved in the music business is to start or own your own business. "I can't imagine anyone wanting to book me, so I'll handle it myself." Or, "My style of music isn't mainstream enough, so I'll go it alone." Or, "I don't know anyone who I could handle working for. I want to be my own boss."

Recommended Action

First, acknowledge that taking risks is tough and not for everyone. Determine what your level of tolerance for risk is in each of the four areas described in Chapter Four: time, money, reputation, and self-esteem. If you can handle "putting everything on the line," then going into business for yourself is viable from a risk standpoint. If you prefer lower stress but still want to be involved in music, look for a job with an existing company or wait for your personal situation or market conditions to change.

APPLYING WHAT YOU'VE LEARNED

We're just about at the end of this book. How do you feel now compared to when you started reading Chapter One? My aim has been to inform and inspire—to provide a set of tools for making good business decisions, constructing a business plan, developing a comprehensive marketing strategy, and setting realistic goals and objectives.

You are now ready to apply what you've learned. Here's a tip: Re-read the "Key Points in This Chapter" at the end of each chapter. You will likely say to yourself, "Now I get it...." From there, go to work.

KEY POINTS IN THIS CHAPTER

1. Lesson 1: "Planning is your first and best business investment." As described throughout this book, doing the planning up front saves time and money. You can't afford not to plan.

2. Lesson 2: "No product sells itself." Beware of the tendency to minimize the role of sales and marketing in your music business. Make sure your sales are handled by someone who likes to sell, knows how to sell, and is properly compensated.

3. Lesson 3: "Artistic integrity and commercial viability are intrinsically compatible." Beware of music industry myths that exaggerate the need to "suffer for the music." You don't have to compromise quality or conform to musical or business stereotypes.

4. Lesson 4: "The biggest marketing challenge is standing out from the competition." Focus on targetable customers as discussed in Chapter Fourteen. Promote positive differentiation between you and your competitors.

5. Mastering time management is essential for success in the music business. Start by understanding that you and your customers have a finite amount of time, attention, and money.

6. Lesson 5: "It's OK to be risk-averse." Your decision to either develop your own music business or work for someone else ties to your feelings about risk. Determine your tolerance level for risk in each of the four areas described in Chapter Four: time, money, reputation, and self-esteem.

7. Make decisions for yourself—don't just "go with the flow." Your situation, like every business situation, is unique. While you can learn from others' successes and failures, it is virtually impossible—and generally not advisable—to simply copy them verbatim.

8. Once again, there are no secrets or gimmicks to business success. Hopefully, applying what you have learned in this book, along with your common sense, can get you further on the road to succeeding in music.

TWO KEY QUESTIONS REVISITED

In Chapter Two, I posed two strategic questions that you should now be able to answer and address fully.

Question 1. What do I want to accomplish?

Assuming that you have articulated your mission, vision, goals, and objectives, you have the answers. It is likely that those answers are now somewhat different from when we first addressed the issue. That's part of life in the music business—things change.

Question 2. How much am I willing to risk?

We talked about the need to understand the risks and rewards inherent in the music business and how they affect your time, money, reputation, and self-esteem. While there is risk in every business situation, you are now equipped to understand and manage risk better than you might have been before reading this book. And as the saying goes, "when in doubt, quantify."

Answering these two questions comes more easily for some people than others. Some either never address the questions, or keep searching for the perfect answers. Trust the process and remember that there is no perfect path or outcome—just ongoing examination, reassessment, and improvement.

I've tried to make it easier for you to create a music business plan that allows you to fully understand what you want to accomplish, what the challenges are in achieving your goals and objectives, and what tools are available to help you control both risks and opportunities. I hope it's been helpful and rewarding for you.

THREE FINAL POINTS

How would I summarize *Succeeding in Music*? Here is the essence:

1. Double the planning time and cut the implementation time in half. This is an old time-management rule of thumb. It's easier and less costly to do the planning up front than to learn everything by trial and error. Construct your business plan early in the game.

2. The biggest challenge is competing for attention. We are continually bombarded with information today, and this is unlikely to change. Remember the absolute necessity of your marketing plan in the overall scheme of things.

3. Someone has to manage the business. If not you, find someone who will. Identify your strengths and weaknesses, and then build your team.

Let me know how things are going. Visit the *Succeeding in Music* website at www.succeedinginmusic.net, and stay in touch. Good luck!

REFERENCE SECTION

Here's additional information that will help you in your quest for success in the business of music. The material in this "workbook" section is organized in three primary areas: sample business plan, worksheets, and resources. Note: All of this material is on the CD-ROM that accompanies this book. You'll be able (with the help of Microsoft Word and Excel) to edit the sample forms and worksheets to suit your needs.

SAMPLE BUSINESS PLAN

We'll re-visit our friends from "The Band Story," give them a name and a fresh start. The business plan includes the following:
- Vision, mission, and values statements
- Brand positioning statement
- Market overview
- Product plan
- Staff and team organization overview
- Operations and infrastructure overview
- Marketing plan including trackable business objectives
- Key milestones for the coming year
- List of basic financials and appendix items

WORKSHEETS AND CHECKLISTS

This section includes blank forms and planning templates from the book:
- Risk analysis checklist
- Business plan contents checklist including appendix items
- The five-year window key objectives matrix

RESOURCES

This section includes information and tools for further study:
- Glossary of key terms, concepts, and buzzwords
- Bibliography: books, magazines, trade associations, and websites
- Contents of the accompanying CD-ROM
- Information on succeedinginmusic.net web community

DISCLAIMER: THE FOLLOWING PEOPLE AND EVENTS DESCRIBED ARE FICTIONAL AND INCLUDED HERE FOR EDUCATIONAL PURPOSES ONLY. ANY RESEMBLANCE TO REAL PEOPLE LIVING OR DEAD IS COINCIDENTAL.

"OUR BAND" BUSINESS PLAN

This is the business plan for Our Band in fiscal years (FY) 2003-2005. The band was founded in 1998 by Ricky and Ronnie Williams to provide an outlet for musical creativity and a source of extra income beyond our day jobs. In the years since, the company has grown, expanded in scope, and performed hundreds of show dates.

This document is the basis for further growth of Our Band's business. It is intended to serve as the foundation for decision-making on all levels: finance, sales, marketing, product development, operations, staff organization, and management. The audience includes Our Band members, staff, and select advisors, and is otherwise confidential.

I. Vision

Changes in musical trends, technology, and culture have had a significant impact on both business and private life. As we look to the future, we envision the following:

- Music will continue to be a significant element of world culture and the entertainment industry. People simply love to listen, dance, and be entertained.
- Individuals (fans) will enjoy a gradually increasing amount of discretionary time, both on and off the job. This puts them in a position to turn to music for entertainment, both live and recorded.
- The music industry will continue to diversify. There is no single "most popular" musical style, as there has not been a "mass market" for some years now. This opens the door to unique musical entertainment and music businesses that did not exist or could not flourish before.

- The business world and the creative world will stabilize its relationship over time. As we learn and develop business skills, business people will come to understand the value of our music and the role of entertainment in daily life.
- The two (business and music) will peacefully coexist. In other words, a music person or group like Our Band does not need to "sell out" (compromise quality) in order to be financially successful.

II. Mission

The mission of Our Band is to enhance the quality of life through music and entertainment. To do this, we strive for the following:

- We write, perform, and record music with positive messages that are meaningful to our target audiences.
- We build our business by charging fair market value for our products.
- We continually invest in the growth of Our Band, our company, and our community.

III. Values

Our values drive our business. Our Band believes the following:

- Music is a universal language that helps performers and their audiences enjoy life more.
- The music business is a people business. It is important to understand and deal with the human factors on all levels, from staff to customers to suppliers.
- Change is a prerequisite for growth. To be better implies being different; being different points to the need for change.
- Being the best in music includes having a unique combination of musical ability, entertainment ability, and common sense business chops. We strive for strength in all three areas.

- Truth and objectivity go hand in hand. Accurate analysis of current and future situations requires steadfast, often brutal honesty. As a result, "the truth shall set you free."
- Personal relationships form the foundation for all business. Computers, factories, offices, and communications equipment are examples of tools for doing business—all operated by real people. Strong relationships make for strong business.
- We learn continually: new material, new licks, new skills. Both knowledge and experience are essential to success. All three—knowledge, experience, and success—increase over time.
- Communication skills form the basis for all success in business and in life. Poor communication ability spells danger. Compromised communication impedes all life functions. Superior communications skills represent a competitive advantage.
- There is an abundance of opportunity and prosperity available to all who view the music business environment that way (as opposed to the scarcity view). We choose to create win-win prosperity scenarios for all our stakeholders rather than view situations as "win-lose" or "zero-sum."

IV. Brand Positioning Statement

Our Band is in the business of providing music and entertainment services on a contract basis. Our clients include promoters, record labels, and fans worldwide. We focus on those customers (promoters and fans) who share our love of dance and pop music of the 1980s and 1990s.

Our fans are motivated by a combination of needs, including:

1. The need for entertainment with positive messages

2. The need to dance as well as listen

3. The need to identify with artists who present a positive image on a consistent basis

We provide our fans with a special blend of cover and original material in both live and recorded performances. We can entertain virtually any audience—young or old, hip or square. We consistently exceed fan and promoter expectations and are uniquely competitive in the following areas:

- Quality of the music. We are expert songwriters, arrangers, and performers. We are well rehearsed and cohesive entertainers.
- Adaptability and flexibility. We integrate easily within each promoter's unique environment. We are versatile and work comfortably in most performance situations.
- Marketing and promotion. We provide high quality promotional materials and participate willingly in interviews and showcases. Our representatives maintain the highest standards of creativity and cooperation in making events successful for promoters and fans alike.
- Attention to detail. We know that the little things count. We take pride in our thoroughness and accuracy in communication, professional image, and follow-up.
- Timeliness and accountability. We show up on time and work within schedules. We understand the time value of money and the monetary value of time, and work closely with our clients to optimize resources.

Promoters and fans regard Our Band as a friend and musical resource. We write, record, and perform—one, two, or all three depending on the situation. While project lengths vary, relationships are long-term.

We are acknowledged by the music industry—clients and competitors alike—as a leading band. Our success is measured in terms of our promoters' ability to make money and our fans' ability to be entertained.

V. The Market Overview

Target Client Profiles

While our fans buy tickets, records, and merchandise, our clients include live music venues, promoters, and record labels. Key segments include:

1. Showcase and dance clubs ranging from 300 to 1,000 seats

2. Promoters of special events in the corporate world: trade shows, special meetings, store openings, etc.

3. College and university activities programs

4. Record labels who focus on danceable pop music and target acts who can sell 10,000 or more records per year

While we have performed for private events (weddings, parties, reunions, etc.) we do not target them in our current marketing efforts.

Our target clients have the following characteristics:

- In business at least two years
- Use our kind of music regularly
- Potential for exceeding the guarantee and increasing fees on repeat engagements
- Properly financed and solid business skills—no hobbyists or sharks
- Demonstrate that they value their customers, employees, and vendors

Market Size and Growth

The live music industry is > $1 billion each year. While there are no specific statistics that break out our target segments, we estimate that there are over 2,000 clubs, 3,000 campuses, and 500 special events promoters who use live dance and pop music each year in North America alone. The total number of show dates promoted is unknown.

The record industry sells an estimated 780 million units per year according to SoundScan.

This market allows for ample growth of Our Band's business for the next three years.

Competitive Environment

The music business has become increasingly competitive since Our Band was founded in 1998. There are more performers and recording artists than ever before, each going after increased sales volume and market share. Direct competitors fall into three categories:

Professional acts. These include other full-time performers and recording artists who do what we do.

"Performing Engineers." These include deejays and mixers who take the place of a live act with "two turntables and a microphone."

Amateur performers. These are "nuisance-factor" competitors who call themselves bands but are really part-time hobbyists.

Indirect competitors include a wide range of entertainment service providers who target the same client profiles as we do. Examples include:

- Sports events and promotions
- Hypnotists, jugglers, and novelty acts
- Karaoke machines
- Movies, theater, and film festivals
- Travel and leisure activities

VI. Product Plan

Over the past five years, Our Band has focused on two primary sources of revenue: live performance fees and record sales. In that time, we have also developed original songs that can potentially be recorded by others.

As we begin to look to the future, we will continue to rely on performing and recording as primary product areas. In addition, we plan to develop the following products:

- Line of merchandise including shirts and novelty items (2003)

- Catalog of original songs to pitch to other artists (2004)
- Fan club with membership revenue through our website (2005)

We also will continue to integrate new cover material into our live shows in addition to original songs.

VII. Our Band Team Organization

Band Members
- Ronnie Williams: co-founder, guitar, vocals, songwriter
- Ricky Williams: co-founder, keyboards, vocals, songwriter
- Jennifer Jackson: bass guitar, vocals, songwriter
- Desmond "Sticks" Cremona: drums, vocals, songwriter
- James Lee: sound engineer, driver, all-around technical guru

Management
General management of Our Band is handled by the two founders, with duties as follows:
- Sales: Ronnie Williams
- Marketing: Ricky Williams
- New product development: Ronnie and Ricky Williams with help from Our Band
- Finance: Ronnie Williams
- Operations (information systems, human resources, facilities): Ricky Williams

See the appendix for brief biographical information on Ronnie and Ricky.

Staff and Vendors
We currently have no staff on the payroll other than the band members mentioned above. Over time, we may add staff in bookkeeping and coordination of communication between the band and the rest of the business team.

The Our Band team is supported by key vendors and subcontractors:
- Booking agent: Richard Adams at Dancemeisters Agency
- Publicist: open
- General legal counsel: Jerry Smith of Smith, Smith, and Smith Attorneys LLC
- Music business and intellectual property attorney: open
- Recording engineer/producer: Mike Fishman
- Home base club: "Gyrations"
- Computer system and mobile communications expert: United Technologies
- Market research and promotional writing: Currently seeking additional vendors
- Accounting and tax advisor: Acme Accounting Services
- Human resources and employee benefits advisor: The HR Company
- Insurance programs: Independent Underwriters Agency
- Financial advisor: open
- Graphic designer: open
- Webmaster: open
- Spiritual advisor and famous chocolate chip cookies: Linda "Mom" Williams

While none of the above are full-time positions, we consider them to be key members of the Our Band team.

VIII. Operations and Infrastructure

Office and Rehearsal Facilities
Our Band sublets two rooms from Ronnie Williams. One room is set up for band business: communications, meetings, files, and storage of promotional materials. The other room is set up for group songwriting, demo recording, and rehearsals.

When we need a full stage and sound system for rehearsals, we use our home club, Gyrations. As our business grows, we plan to move more of the business functions out of the Williams household and into the offices of our team members.

Information Systems

Our Band members are equipped with computers. This allows each member to create song files as well as business documents and share them easily.

- Each band member is equipped with a tested, reliable, full-featured computer, printer, and software.
- Stations are wired to the Internet via always-on DSL service.
- Software allows us to read and write in both Macintosh and Windows platforms.

Special Equipment and Technology

Since we are active in the music industry, we are conscious of and have access to a wide range of instruments and equipment. In addition to basic computers and telephones, Our Band's offices include:

- Audio/video playback systems with capability to reproduce most media formats, including DVD, DAT, VHS, audio cassette, audio CD, phonograph, and standard radio and television
- Communications tools including multi-line telephones with conference and speaker phone features, fax machine, mobile telephones, and caller ID
- CD burners capable of duplicating data and music disks
- Scanner

Band members own and maintain their personal instruments and stage rigs. The company owns a basic sound reinforcement system and uses house systems for most shows. The rehearsal room is equipped with a basic demo recording system. We use other recording equipment owned by Mike Fishman and other studios that we use from time to time.

IX. Marketing Plan

As we look to the years ahead, some aspects of the marketing mix will stay the same, some will change, and some will be added. This section describes how we will market over the next three years.

Product Concepts and Rationale

Emphasis in 2003 will be in two primary areas:

- Personal appearances ranging from $1,500–$2,500 per day—our "bread and butter."
- Record sales including one new release added to our current catalog of two prior records.

Future revenue streams include:

- Royalties and advances. To date we have produced and merchandised our own records. We plan to look for a record label in 2003 and hope to sign a deal by the end of the year.
- Merchandise sales. We plan to offer a line of T-shirts and Our Band logo novelty items for sale at shows. We'll introduce this late in 2003.
- Fan club. We've developed a mailing list of over 6,500 fans who have either attended shows or bought records over the past two years. We plan to develop this into a membership organization with its own marketing plan in 2004 for launch in 2005.

Key Product Benefits

Our fans and promoter clients look to us for the following benefits:

For Fans

- Exciting shows. Instrumentally, vocally, and visually, we put on a great show. Fans are energized and entertained.
- Positive messages. Our lyrics and image are upbeat without being sentimental. People have a good time and forget their troubles when they listen to our songs.
- Consistency. We're there for our fans and keep coming back to entertain. They can count on us to deliver. We want you to be a fan for life.

For Promoters

- Spending crowds. We draw people who buy tickets and like to party. They buy food, beverages, and merchandise in addition to show tickets and cover charges.
- Promotional support. We provide photos, press materials, and records as part of our standard package. This puts our promoter clients in a position to market our shows more competitively.
- Empathy. We understand enough about the music business to understand what our customers are going through. Offstage, we talk their language and can relate to their situation enough to form lasting business and personal relationships.

Our Unique Competitive Advantage

Our Band is one of the few groups of its kind that offers both musical and business integrity. Our musical ability is complemented by our team's business chops. This unique combination of musicianship and professionalism helps us stand out from our competitors in a positive way.

Essence of Our Band's Marketing Strategy

In 2003 and beyond, we will focus on three primary marketing and sales initiatives:

1. Upgrade the presentation package. We are investing in updates and enhancements to our website, brochure, and other collateral material. We will have a new photo and press kit done, updating the last one that was done in 2000.

2. Find a record label. We will continue to sell our self-produced records, and use them to establish a label relationship by the end of 2003. This goes along with the development of new collateral materials.

3. Use merchandise for revenue in addition to promotion. We have given away limited runs of Our Band T-shirts in the past. As our fan base, web presence, and record sales grow, we will add the sale of logo identity items to our revenue base.

Note: Preliminary "how-to's" for each of the above are included in the tactical marketing plan below.

Pricing and Financial Assumptions

1. Personal appearances are based on daily performance rates.

- Average club rate: $1,500
- Average campus or corporate rate: $2,500

2. Expenses are not reimbursed by clients. Our fees need to cover travel and overhead in addition to personal compensation.

3. Selling price for records is $15 each, including postage and handling. We only sell direct to fans.

4. Bookkeeping is done on a cash basis.

5. We meet monthly to review results and adjust forecasts and tactical plans to reflect current reality.

6. The fiscal calendar is January 1–December 31.

Key Metrics: Trackable Business Objectives

	FY 03	FY 04	FY 05
• Performance revenue	$425K	$500K	$650K
• Fixed marketing expense budget	$35K	$40K	$50K
• Number of personal appearances	200	210	220
• Records sold	7,000	12,000	25,000
• Records in our catalog	2	3	4
• Mailing list	7,500	10,000	15,000
• Fan club members	N/A	N/A	2,000
• Number of publicity hits/reviews	20	30	50

Tactical Marketing Methods

1. Essence of the selling strategy

- Continue to work with Dancemeisters to sell increasingly high-quality dates. Support them with the new press kit and mailing list.
- Focus on corporate parties as better paying gigs than private parties.
- Find a record label in 2003 so we can record a new album in 2004.

2. Product mix

- Live performance fees are the foundation of our revenue.
- Increase record sales as a percentage of total band business.
- Plan for merchandise line in 2004 and fan club in 2005.

See the sales budget in the appendix for detail on sales by product and client category.

3. Pricing model and strategy

Our rates are in the middle of the high end in our part of the country. We are able to get a little more per date than competitors because of our draw and exciting shows. We plan to increase prices as we record more and develop our mailing list into a fan club.

4. Promotion plan.

Forecasted promotional expenses are included in the fixed marketing expenses budget in the appendix. Key elements of the promotion plan are listed below.

- *Advertising media.* We do not advertise directly, but we supply photos, bios, and support materials to promoters, who can use those materials in their advertising and promotion.
- *Publicity.* Work with Dancemeisters' publicist to develop a new press kit based on updated collateral package. Send press releases on key showcase dates and growth of the band to the music trades as part of the effort to locate a record label.
- *Sales literature.* Update the current brochure, press kit, photos, and collateral package in the first quarter of 2003.
- *Demo recordings and other collateral material.* Use our latest record ("Live at McDill's") in lieu of auditions and for in-club promotion.
- *Direct marketing.* Continue "Our Band Notes" newsletter series two times in 2003. Include order forms for records with each mailing. Start to make the newsletter interactive with a fax-back survey.

- *Trade shows and special events.* Attend the *Billboard* Magazine Dance Summit and *Keyboard* Magazine "Keyboard Day" events in 2003.
- *Key influencer relations.* Leverage our relationship with the Rockin' 80s Band to get an introduction to Pop King Records.
- *Wearables and identity items.* Produce a gift for key clients and record label prospects in the third quarter of 2003. May accompany holiday greetings sent in the fourth quarter. Use T-shirts and other merchandise for promotion as well as for sale.
- *Showcase performances.* Showcase at the National Association for Campus Activities convention to help secure premium college dates. Do two local benefit concerts in our home club and invite the press and prospective corporate event planners as our guests.
- *Website and e-commerce.* Upgrade our website to allow online record orders. Send special newsletter to fan base with e-mail addresses in addition to traditional "snail mail" newsletter.

5. Geographical territory

Most performing work is done in a 200-mile radius of our home base. That way we can drive to all gigs, and focus promotional efforts regionally until we record for a label with national distribution.

6. Salesforce strategy

Sales of show dates are handled by Richard Adams at Dancemeisters Agency for clubs, colleges, and corporate events. Ronnie Williams is the band contact for sales, and responsible for heading up our quest for a record label.

7. Attractive end-user segments

- College campuses with 1,000 to 5,000 students. We can position ourselves as "stars" on the medium-sized campuses.
- Dance and show clubs with 500 to 1,000 capacity. The size means that we can command a larger fee while not competing with national touring acts. In some of the larger clubs, we can share the bill or open for name acts.
- Corporate event planners in low-tech industries. We go over great at parties and store openings in the fashion retail, automotive, and fast food world.

While we have done work with small clubs and private parties in the past, we do not target them for future growth.

8. Direct competitors

- Dance bands, including the Rave Mongers, Dancing Beasts, and Banyan Tree
- Performing engineers and deejays including Steve Wilson, Mister Twister, and Tofu Berger
- Weekend warriors including The Garage Band, The Amy Phillips Trio, and Bar and the Dogs

Schedule of Key
Milestones for 2003–2005

(Note: Q1, Q2, Q3, and Q4 refer to the first, second, third, and fourth quarters of the year.)

Q1 2003

- Upgrade photos, press kits, and sales materials
- Q1 revenue = $95K

Q2 2003

- Our Band Notes issue #5
- Q2 revenue = $100K

Q3 2003

- Develop new T-shirt and merchandise line
- Play first $5,000 gig at sales meeting for corporate client
- Q3 revenue = $120K

Q4 2003

- Our Band Notes issue #6
- Holiday package to promoters and vendors including logo gift item
- Secure record deal
- Q4 revenue = $110K
- Total year performance revenue = $425K
- Total record revenue = $85K
- Total merchandise revenue = $10K
- Grand total revenue = $520K
- Band members quit day jobs (finally!)

2004

- Record and release new record with nationally distributed label
- Average gig price > $2,000
- Total performance revenue = $500K
- Total record revenue = $130K
- Total merchandise revenue = $50K
- Grand total revenue = $680K

2005

- Launch Our Band Fan Club
- Average gig price > $3,000
- Total performance revenue = $650K
- Total record revenue = $250K (includes advance, royalties, and direct sales)
- Total merchandise revenue = $100K
- Grand total revenue = $1,000K (Wow, that's a million bucks!)

X. Financials

Detailed financial schedules are included in the appendix section as follows:

Revenue plan and key objectives FY (fiscal year) 2003-05

P&L / expense budgets FY 2003-05

Detailed fixed marketing expense budget FY 2003-05

New equipment priorities FY 2003

XI. Contents of Appendix

A. Organization chart and team contact list

B. Job descriptions and band bios

C. Master client history spreadsheet ranked by total sales

D. Product plan spreadsheet and tracking matrix FY 2001-05

E. Historical data: FY 2002 final reports

F. Sample promotion materials including newsletter and press clippings

WORKSHEETS AND CHECKLISTS

Here are blank worksheets that will help you develop your business plan. Electronic versions are included on the CD-ROM.

Risk Analysis Checklist

Answer the following questions, knowing that you are the only judge. The more yes answers you have, the more prepared you are to take the risk of going into the music business for yourself.

The market is big enough to support my music business; people are ready to buy what I'm selling.

     Yes   No

I understand my competitors (direct and indirect) and can differentiate myself from them.

     Yes   No

I know who will handle each of the key elements of my business: sales, marketing, accounting and finance, operations, product development, and general management.

     Yes   No

I have a written business plan that looks three years into the future.

     Yes   No

I have sources of funding to cover my business and personal expenses for one year or more.

     Yes   No

My risk tolerance is high.

     Yes   No

Best case scenario is that you answered "yes" to all six questions. If not, go back and see what it would take to do so. You are probably closer than you think.

Business Plan Contents Checklist

Use this section as a guide and checklist to be sure that you have thought through and written down all the elements of your business plan.

Vision, Mission, and Values Statement

We believe that the future of our business is bright because:

_____

_____

_____

_____

We are in business to:

_____

_____

_____

_____

We believe in the following business values and operating principles:

_____

_____

_____

_____

Brand Positioning Statement

The brand positioning statement is the foundation of your marketing plan and clearly establishes how you are different from your competitors. It is a one-page document that answers the following four questions accurately and succinctly: Use this page as a worksheet, then refine from there.

What business are we in?

_____

_____

_____

_____

Who are our customers?

_____

_____

_____

_____

What makes us special?

_____

_____

_____

_____

What's in it for everybody (customers, vendors, community, owner/investors, us)?

_____

_____

_____

_____

The Three-Year Product Plan

Your products (goods and services) are what your customers pay you for. Whether you are a performer, songwriter, agent, manager, or promoter, you are likely to sell more than one category of product. In addition, your product mix is likely to change over time. Use this worksheet to think through the products you plan to offer over the next three years. Start by filling in what you are already offering in the "Last Year" and "This Year" columns.

Product	Last Year	This Year	Next Year	Year Two	Year Three

Operational Elements

Creating the product is important, but delivering it consistently and profitably points to your business's operations, or ability to execute the plan. Think through each of the following, and estimate costs and time needed. Use this worksheet as a quick start and checklist. Create financial spreadsheets and other documentation as your business plan comes together.

	Estimated Cost $	Who's Responsible	Deadline Date
Location (workspace) and infrastructure			
Licenses and business registration/incorporation			
Staff organizations and benefits			
Marketing plan			
Accounting and success measurement			

The Detailed Operating Plan Document Package

Once you've got the first three elements—mission, brand positioning statement, and product strategy—you are in a position to create an operating plan. This is the part of the plan that most people think of when they think of a business plan. Let's make a distinction here. Remember the definition of strategy vs. tactics? A strategy is a decision. A tactic is a method. In a strategic business plan, *both*—strategies and tactics—are articulated.

Organize all of the above financial information and other documentation into a concise written plan. Note: Taking this step assumes that you have decided to start the business. Elements of the plan include:

1. Detailed revenue forecast. Revenue = units sold x average selling price, by product and by month.

2. Marketing plan. Use the marketing plan outline from the sample business plan for "Our Band" to guide you.

3. Budgets and pro forma financials. These are the hardcore financial schedules, related to both income (revenue forecast) and expenses in all areas. The words "pro forma" come from Latin and imply that portions of the material are hypothetical (future) as opposed to actual (real history). Examples of financial material include departmental or project expense budgets, income or profit and loss ("P&L") statements, and balance sheets.

4. Organization plan. This includes a listing of each staff position, the reporting structure (best illustrated in a graphical organization chart), job descriptions for each position, and a description of employee benefits provided by the company. Benefits include: (1) insurance (health, life, disability, liability), (2) paid holiday schedule, vacation, and personal-day policies, (3) retirement, profit sharing, or stock options, and (4) any extras not covered elsewhere such as day care, fitness counseling, on-the-job training, or tuition reimbursement.

5. Capital purchase schedule. Capital purchases are those items which the company buys that have a useful life of longer than one year. In most cases, the Internal Revenue Service requires that capital purchases be depreciated, that is deducted from taxable revenue over the useful life of the item rather than all at once. Examples include vehicles (cars, vans, trucks, buses), equipment (like stage gear, instruments, and recording equipment), and real estate.

6. Appendix items or supplemental material. The plan document should include material that illuminates the text and numbers without cluttering things up. You decide what items are most important for your purpose. Examples include:

- Organization chart
- Job descriptions and consultant bios
- Information policy
- Master client history spreadsheet ranked by total sales
- Product plan spreadsheet
- Historical data: prior years' financial reports
- Customer profiles and target customer criteria
- Sample promotion materials, press clippings, awards, website content
- Employee handbook including company policies and benefits
- Market research reports and statistics
- Detailed profiles of competitors

Goals and Objectives: The Five-Year Window

What gets measured, gets done. The following worksheets are a place for you to log in your key goals and objectives in the three categories discussed in Chapter Fifteen. Remember that goals are long-term desired results. Objectives are aspects of goals that are specific, measurable, and achievable. As such, list your goals first, without time constraints. Then break them down into trackable objectives, looking three years into the future. These worksheets are also included on the CD-ROM.

Top Five Creative Goals

1 _____

2 _____

3 _____

4 _____

5 _____

Creative Objectives	Last Year	This Year	Next Year	Year 2	Year 3
Songs written by me					
Songs written and recorded by me					
My songs recorded by others					
Records released					
New material in stage show					
Music association award					
Grammy award					
Other award					
News/press clippings in trade media					
News/press clippings in general media					
Radio airplay					
Radio interviews/appearances					
Television airplay					
Television interviews/appearances					
Record reviews					
Song reviews					
Largest venue I performed in					
Smallest venue I performed in					
Largest audience					
Smallest audience					
Fan testimonials					
Promoter testimonials					
Competitive testimonials					
Number of fan club members					
Website unique visitors					
Benefits or pro bono shows					

Top Five Financial Goals

1 _____

2 _____

3 _____

4 _____

5 _____

Financial Objectives	Last Year	This Year	Next Year	Year 2	Year 3
Songs recorded by me or others					
Average royalty income per song					
Total royalty revenue					
Smallest revenue for one song					
Largest revenue for one song					
Records sold—all titles in release					
Average royalty or margin per record					
Total revenue from record sales					
Smallest revenue from one record					
Largest revenue from one record					
Number of show dates performed					
Average revenue per show date					
Total live performance revenue					
Smallest revenue from one show date					
Largest revenue from one show date					
Product endorsement revenue					
Corporate sponsorship revenue					
Merchandising and other revenue					
Grand Total Revenue $					
Allowance for Expenses $ (50%)					
Left Over to Pay People $					
Number of People					
Average Share $					
Target Average Share $					
Variance $					

Top Five Personal Goals

1. _____

2. _____

3. _____

4. _____

5. _____

Personal Objectives	Last Year	This Year	Next Year	Year 2	Year 3
Number of days worked	_____	_____	_____	_____	_____
Average revenue per day	_____	_____	_____	_____	_____
Number of hours worked	_____	_____	_____	_____	_____
Average revenue per hour	_____	_____	_____	_____	_____

Vacation objective: **Last year:** _____

This year: _____

Next year: _____

Year 2: _____

Year 3: _____

Family objective: **Last year:** _____

This year: _____

Next year: _____

Year 2: _____

Year 3: _____

Community Objective: **Last year:** _____

This year: _____

Next year: _____

Year 2: _____

Year 3: _____

Spiritual objective: **Last year:** _____

This year: _____

Next year: _____

Year 2: _____

Year 3: _____

Educational objective: Last year: _____

This year: _____

Next year: _____

Year 2: _____

Year 3: _____

Health objective: Last year: _____

This year: _____

Next year: _____

Year 2: _____

Year 3: _____

Exercise and fitness objective: Last year: _____

This year: _____

Next year: _____

Year 2: _____

Year 3: _____

Hobby and recreational objective: Last year: _____

This year: _____

Next year: _____

Year 2: _____

Year 3: _____

Other personal objective: Last year: _____

This year: _____

Next year: _____

Year 2: _____

Year 3: _____

Top Five Creative Goals

1 _____

2 _____

3 _____

4 _____

5 _____

Creative Objectives	Last Year	This Year	Next Year	Year 2	Year 3
Songs written by represented artists					
Songs recorded by represented artists					
Songs recorded by others					
Records released by represented artists					
New acts represented					
IBMA awards won by represented acts					
Grammy awards won by represented acts					
Other awards					
News/press clippings in trade media					
News/press clippings in general media					
Radio airplay					
Radio interviews/appearances					
Television airplay					
Television interviews/appearances					
Record reviews					
Song reviews					
Largest venue acts performed in					
Smallest venue acts performed in					
Largest audience					
Smallest audience					
Fan testimonials					
Promoter testimonials					
Competitive testimonials					
Number of fan club members					
Website unique visitors					
Benefits or pro bono shows					

Top Five Financial Goals

1 _____

2 _____

3 _____

4 _____

5 _____

Financial Objectives	Last Year	This Year	Next Year	Year 2	Year 3
Songs recorded by represented artists	_____	_____	_____	_____	_____
Average royalty income per song	_____	_____	_____	_____	_____
Total royalty revenue	_____	_____	_____	_____	_____
Smallest revenue for one song	_____	_____	_____	_____	_____
Largest revenue for one song	_____	_____	_____	_____	_____
Commission %—song royalties	_____	_____	_____	_____	_____
Total commission $—song royalties	_____	_____	_____	_____	_____
Records sold by all artists represented	_____	_____	_____	_____	_____
Average royalty or margin per record	_____	_____	_____	_____	_____
Total revenue from record sales	_____	_____	_____	_____	_____
Smallest revenue from one record	_____	_____	_____	_____	_____
Largest revenue from one record	_____	_____	_____	_____	_____
Commission %—record revenue	_____	_____	_____	_____	_____
Total commission $—record revenue	_____	_____	_____	_____	_____
Number of show dates booked	_____	_____	_____	_____	_____
Average revenue per show date	_____	_____	_____	_____	_____
Total live performance revenue	_____	_____	_____	_____	_____
Smallest revenue from one show date	_____	_____	_____	_____	_____
Largest revenue from one show date	_____	_____	_____	_____	_____
Commission %—live shows	_____	_____	_____	_____	_____
Total commission $—live shows	_____	_____	_____	_____	_____
Product endorsement revenue	_____	_____	_____	_____	_____
Corporate sponsorship revenue	_____	_____	_____	_____	_____
Merchandising and other revenue	_____	_____	_____	_____	_____
Commission %—other revenue	_____	_____	_____	_____	_____
Total commission $—other revenue	_____	_____	_____	_____	_____
Grand Total Commission	_____	_____	_____	_____	_____
Revenue $	_____	_____	_____	_____	_____
Allowance for Expenses $ (50%)	_____	_____	_____	_____	_____
Left Over to Pay People $	_____	_____	_____	_____	_____
Number of People	_____	_____	_____	_____	_____
Average Share $	_____	_____	_____	_____	_____
Target Average Share $	_____	_____	_____	_____	_____
Variance $	_____	_____	_____	_____	_____

Top Five Personal Goals

1 _____

2 _____

3 _____

4 _____

5 _____

Personal Objectives	Last Year	This Year	Next Year	Year 2	Year 3
Number of days worked	_____	_____	_____	_____	_____
Average revenue per day	_____	_____	_____	_____	_____
Number of hours worked	_____	_____	_____	_____	_____
Average revenue per hour	_____	_____	_____	_____	_____

Vacation objective: **Last year:** _____

This year: _____

Next year: _____

Year 2: _____

Year 3: _____

Family objective: **Last year:** _____

This year: _____

Next year: _____

Year 2: _____

Year 3: _____

Community Objective: **Last year:** _____

This year: _____

Next year: _____

Year 2: _____

Year 3: _____

Spiritual objective: **Last year:** _____

This year: _____

Next year: _____

Year 2: _____

Year 3: _____

Educational objective: **Last year:** _____

This year: _____

Next year: _____

Year 2: _____

Year 3: _____

Health objective: **Last year:** _____

This year: _____

Next year: _____

Year 2: _____

Year 3: _____

Exercise and fitness objective: **Last year:** _____

This year: _____

Next year: _____

Year 2: _____

Year 3: _____

Hobby and recreational objective: **Last year:** _____

This year: _____

Next year: _____

Year 2: _____

Year 3: _____

Other personal objective **Last year:** _____

This year: _____

Next year: _____

Year 2: _____

Year 3: _____

Top Five Creative Goals

1 _____

2 _____

3 _____

4 _____

5 _____

Creative Objectives	Last Year	This Year	Next Year	Year 2	Year 3
Repeat acts presented					
New acts presented					
Total acts presented					
Regular recurring events—clubs					
Special events—concerts					
Special events—festivals					
Special events—corporate or private					
Other events type:					
News/press clippings in trade media					
News/press clippings in general media					
Radio airplay					
Radio interviews/appearances					
Television airplay					
Television interviews/appearances					
Concert/event reviews					
Largest venue I presented in					
Smallest venue I presented in					
Largest audience—single-day event					
Smallest audience—single-day event					
Largest audience—multiple-day event					
Smallest audience—multiple-day event					
Fan testimonials					
Performer testimonials					
Agent/manager testimonials					
Competitive testimonials					
Number of VIP club members					
Website unique visitors					
Benefits or pro bono shows					

Top Five Financial Goals

1 _____

2 _____

3 _____

4 _____

5 _____

Financial Objectives	Last Year	This Year	Next Year	Year 2	Year 3
Number of events—single date					
Average number of tickets sold					
Average ticket price $					
Average revenue per single date					
Subtotal ticket revenue					
Smallest revenue from one show date					
Largest revenue from one show date					
Number of events—multiple date					
Average number of tickets sold					
Average ticket price $					
Average revenue per single date					
Subtotal ticket revenue					
Smallest revenue from one event					
Largest revenue from one event					
Product endorsement revenue					
Corporate sponsorship revenue					
Merchandising and other revenue					
Grand Total Revenue $					
Allowance for Expenses $ (50%)					
Left Over to Pay People $					
Number of People					
Average Share $					
Target Average Share $					
Variance $					

Top Five Personal Goals

1 _____

2 _____

3 _____

4 _____

5 _____

Personal Objectives	Last Year	This Year	Next Year	Year 2	Year 3
Number of days worked	_____	_____	_____	_____	_____
Average revenue per day	_____	_____	_____	_____	_____
Number of hours worked	_____	_____	_____	_____	_____
Average revenue per hour	_____	_____	_____	_____	_____

Vacation objective: **Last year:** _____

This year: _____

Next year: _____

Year 2: _____

Year 3: _____

Family objective: **Last year:** _____

This year: _____

Next year: _____

Year 2: _____

Year 3: _____

Community Objective: **Last year:** _____

This year: _____

Next year: _____

Year 2: _____

Year 3: _____

Spiritual objective: **Last year:** _____

This year: _____

Next year: _____

Year 2: _____

Year 3: _____

Educational objective: Last year: _____

This year: _____

Next year: _____

Year 2: _____

Year 3: _____

Health objective: Last year: _____

This year: _____

Next year: _____

Year 2: _____

Year 3: _____

Exercise and fitness objective: Last year: _____

This year: _____

Next year: _____

Year 2: _____

Year 3: _____

Hobby and recreational objective: Last year: _____

This year: _____

Next year: _____

Year 2: _____

Year 3: _____

Other personal objective: Last year: _____

This year: _____

Next year: _____

Year 2: _____

Year 3: _____

Sources of Working Capital (cash to fund the business)

When you start a business, there is seldom enough revenue from sales operations to cover initial expenses and the costs involved in growth. Many businesses fail because they cannot cover expenses in the early days. Identify in advance where your working capital will come from.

Funding Source	Year One	Year Two	Year Three
Savings			
401(k)/IRA			
Sale of assets: real estate			
Second mortgage			
Credit card cash advance			
"Rich uncle" (friends and relatives)			
Bank loan			
Private investor or "angel"			
Re-invested profits (your businesss)			
Other			

RESOURCES

Glossary of Key Terms, Concepts, and Buzzwords

Here are the most important words and phrases used in this book, presented here in alphabetical order for quick reference.

Advertising: the act of delivering a paid promotional message to a target audience. A key word here is "paid." You pay someone to deliver the message to a predetermined or target audience on your behalf.

Amateur: no compensation—a labor of love.

Art: human expression in sensuous form, often "for its own sake." The word "expression" is very important, because it implies that the motivation comes from within the artist rather than somewhere else.

Assumption: the answer to the question, "How did you get the numbers?" Assumptions are key elements in business plans, as they illuminate and rationalize sales forecasts and expense budgets.

Audience: whoever enjoys the music, whether they are the paying customers or not. Fans who buy tickets are customers of the promoter, but they are the audience for the performer.

Balance sheet: a financial schedule listing a company's assets, liabilities, and stockholder equity. Also known as a "net-worth statement."

Branding: the creation of indelible images (logos, trademarks, messages) of you and your products in the minds of your target customers, audience, and stakeholders. Examples of music business brands include your name or stage name, your company name, names of songs, records, festivals, concert series, clubs, and other venues.

Budget: planned revenue and expenses tracked over time; usually presented in monthly increments over a 12-month fiscal year.

Business plan: a written system of documents that puts your business and its market environment in context over the next several years. It describes what you are going to do, how you are going to do it, and what the consequences are.

Buyer characteristics: common traits that make up the profile of your target customer. Categories of traits include demographic, economic, geographic, and psychographic attributes. This information is used to match the target customer with your product.

Career: business activity or occupation; something done to make a living.

Collateral materials (also referred to simply as "collateral"): those promotional items that work with, but do not take the place of, basic print sales literature. Examples include demo recordings, itineraries, publicity reprints, photos, biographies, agency rosters, etc.

Commerce: buying and selling of goods and services. This implies financial transactions, which further implies a profit motive.

Competitive intelligence system: a set of information that allows you to understand what is going on in the market, and how you and your competitors are dealing with market conditions. Most market information is readily accessible and relatively inexpensive.

Corporation: a legal classification of business for a company with any number of owners (as few as one) that is organized according to laws and tax codes designed to regulate larger firms. The various owners take shares of stock in the company, and that stock can be bought and sold periodically by the individuals with little or no disruption to the business.

Creative goals: the desired long-term results, whether you make money from them or not. Also called artistic goals, they define the business playing field before adding the economic elements. Must be congruent with financial and personal goals.

Customer: whoever pays you directly; where the money changes hands. For example, if a club owner pays a band to perform, the club owner is the customer. If a band pays an agent to secure the booking, the band is the customer.

Day job: what you do outside of music (whether done during the day or at night) to make money to support your musical interests.

Demographic information: age, gender, marital status, and education level of target buyers. Relevant to the creation of buyer profiles.

Differentiation: a pricing and positioning strategy in which the supplier charges as high a price as possible, based on the product's features and competitive advantages. Assumes that there are aspects of each competitor's product that can be distinguished easily and are worth paying more for. This is the most common music industry approach.

Direct competition: competition from similar businesses in the same product category. Examples include other performers, songwriters, booking agents, managers, event promoters, etc.

Direct marketing: any promotional activity in which direct contact is made with the target customer. Also called direct response marketing, it allows you to get relatively immediate and trackable feedback from your target customers. Common techniques include direct mail, telemarketing, and cold canvassing (also called missionary selling).

E-commerce (also called e-business): the process of using the Internet for business. Examples include posting information on websites, e-mail promotion, conducting surveys, or selling merchandise online.

Economic information: household income levels and discretionary spending ability or "buying power" for individuals. Relevant to the creation of buyer profiles.

Elevator test: the challenge of articulating the essence of your brand positioning statement to a stranger in the time it takes to travel ten floors on an elevator. This is a good barometer of how clearly you can describe what you do professionally.

Entertainment: amusement or diversion including public performances or shows. Entertainment—including music—is usually created with the needs of the audience in mind, first and foremost.

Executive summary: a one- or two-page document that includes the essence of the whole business plan. Helpful when seeking financing, especially when many people are reviewing the plan.

Financial goals: the set of desired long-term results that are measured in financial terms. Must be congruent with creative and personal goals.

Full-time: geared to making 100% of financial income; implies focus and dedication.

Geographic information: where your customers physically live or conduct business. Relevant to the creation of buyer profiles.

Goal: a desired result; often long-term. Something good that you aspire to over a long period of time.

Hobby: leisure-time activity; something done for fun.

Hybrid: a pricing and positioning strategy in which the supplier offers more than one product and uses both the low cost producer and differentiation strategies selectively. Some products may be viewed as "commodities" and subject to competitive market pressures; others can be "differentiated" and priced accordingly.

Identity item: the generic term for tangible promotional gifts that include your identity (name, logo, message) and have some usefulness or intrinsic value beyond pure promotion. Also called "advertising specialties," "tschotschkes," or "swag." Examples include wearables (T-shirts, jackets), non-wearables (key rings, guitar picks), and edibles (hot sauce, candy, etc.).

Income statement: a financial schedule which includes a summary of revenue minus expenses, resulting in net income (profit or loss) for a given time period (typically a fiscal year). Also called "P & L," short for profit and loss statement.

Independent or "Indie" label: a record label not owned or exclusively distributed by one of the major label groups.

Indirect competition: competition from any product that goes after the same target customer's attention and money. Examples include not only the obvious entertainment specialists (games, cinema, sports, etc.), but alternative purchases like furniture, clothing, home improvements, computers, cars, and/or activities like vacations, hobbies, and education.

Individual customers: those who make the decision to buy on their own and are usually spending their own money. Examples include clubs or other venues where the owner books the acts, Indie labels or publishing companies run by the owner, and the general ticket- and record-buying public.

Influencers: people who do not buy from you, but can influence your target customers. Examples include managers, record label personnel, celebrity endorsers, and any other source of referrals or recommendations.

Institutional customers: those who make buying decisions in groups and are often spending an organization's money. Examples include college and university "activities committees," major corporate record labels and publishing companies, and ticket brokers and resellers.

Limited Liability Company (LLC) and Limited Liability Partnership (LLP): legal classifications of businesses in which the owners' liability for the financial and legal obligations of the company are protected by the partnership agreement, without some of the administrative detail involved in a full corporation. The partners get the liability protection of a corporation with the tax advantages and simplicity of a partnership.

Links in the marketing chain: the seven elements or links of any marketing plan are: product strategy, pricing strategy, promotional strategy, sales channel strategy, salesforce strategy, customer profiles, and competitive environment.

Low-cost producer: a pricing and positioning strategy in which the supplier prices to the low end of the market and earns acceptable profits by controlling internal costs. This is more relevant to manufacturing and retailing than to the music industry, but still an important concept to understand.

Major label: a record label owned or exclusively distributed by one of the Big Five label groups, including BMG Entertainment, EMI Music, Sony Music Entertainment, Universal Music Group, and Warner Music Group.

Management: the professional administration of any business, even a one-person operation. Management has four key responsibilities: planning, organizing, motivating, and controlling.

Marketing: the act of developing products and exposing them for sale to a specified customer base. Be sure to differentiate marketing from sales, and to understand that marketing has seven key components or "links"—not just advertising and promotion.

Marketing functions: the four functions of marketing in any business are: product planning and positioning, communications and public relations, customer relationship management, and advertising and promotion.

Market segmentation: the process of organizing your approach to target customers for the sake of focus and efficiency. Think of a segment as a "slice of the pie." Music market segmentation is oriented towards styles or genres, but can also be broken down by demographics, economics, geography, and psychographics.

Mission statement: a few sentences or a paragraph that answers the question, "Why are you in business?" This is a key foundation of strategic planning.

Objective: an aspect or subset of a goal that is specific, measurable, and achievable.

Opportunities: environmental trends (both internal and external) with potentially positive consequences, such as a competitive advantage or improved business performance (increased efficiency, sales, profits, or market share).

Part-time: dividing time and focus among various pursuits or sources of income.

Partnership: a legal classification of business in which more than one person owns the company, but it is not set up as a corporation. The partners share the assets and liabilities and are taxed on their share of net company income.

Personal goals: the set of desired long-term results that relate to your health, family, education, recreation, and spiritual pursuits. Must be congruent with creative and financial goals.

Place strategy: the decision about where you conduct business. There are three dimensions of place to consider: geographical territory, channel of distribution or venue type, and your physical workspace.

Planning flow: the concept of doing business planning in a structured sequence to optimize results. The recommended sequence is:

(1) vision, mission, and values statements, (2) brand positioning statement, (3) product plan, (4) detailed operating plan, and (5) daily action list.

Product: what you get paid for—whether goods, services, or a combination. Most businesses offer more than one product, like a performer who gets paid for live performances and record royalties.

Product development: the process of getting the product ready to offer to your target customer base, like rehearsing before going on stage or into the studio.

Product life cycle: each product has a "life cycle" roughly analogous to that of human life, from conception and birth to death. The business world organizes the product life cycle into six phases: research and development, introduction, early growth, late growth or shake-out, maturity or saturation, and decline.

Professional: declared intent to work for pay. May require special training or certification by a third party.

Profit: revenue minus expenses, or the money left over after a business pays the costs of doing business.

Promotional toolbox: a set of tools for building your brand. Examples include advertising, publicity, sales literature, demo recordings, showcase performances, websites, newsletters, identity items, and related materials.

Psychographic information: what your customers think about and believe. This includes social traits, religious or spiritual beliefs, political views, and personal interests. Relevant to the creation of buyer profiles.

Public company or publicly traded company: a classification of business corporation in which anyone qualified to buy stock can be an owner. Public companies are heavily regulated by the government and subject to strict reporting and disclosure procedures.

Publicity: the act of delivering an unpaid educational message to a target audience. The key words here are "unpaid" and "educational." While you pay for advertising space or time, you do not pay for editorial placement of publicity.

Revenue: money coming in to your business, calculated as units sold x average selling price.

Revenue stream: where the money comes from. Agent example: commissions from booked shows represent a revenue stream.

Risk: the danger of loss or other negative consequences. In business, the four things at risk are money, time, reputation, and self-esteem.

Risk analysis: the process of determining what is at risk, and how much risk you are willing and able to take.

Sales: the act of causing and expediting a purchase at a specified price, or within a price range. Be sure to understand the difference between sales and marketing, and how the two work together to achieve business objectives.

Sales functions: the four functions of sales in any business are: achieving sales objectives ("hitting the numbers"), event participation, territory management, and general sales administration.

Sales literature: the brochures and catalogs that describe and depict your product. This is the tangible print material you can deliver to prospective customers via mail, online, or in person.

Self-expression: conveyance of personal feeling, as in art. This implies that the feelings, emotions, and personal needs of the artist (composer, songwriter, performer, producer) take the highest priority.

Showcase performance: a live performance by a solo musician or an entire act in front of someone who might hire them. Demo recordings—especially video—have streamlined this audition process recently.

Sole proprietorship: a legal classification of business, in which one person owns the company. There is no "stock" as in corporations, so the stock cannot be traded.

Strategy: a decision made now that affects future activities. A strategy is a thought process leading to a decision and commitment, not necessarily the behavior or work itself.

Strengths: superior resources and skills that can be drawn on to exploit opportunities and deal with threats.

Supply and demand: the business principle that asserts that selling prices go up or down based on the balance between *supply*, or product availability, and *demand*, or number of potential customers.

"SWOT analysis": a planning tool used to take a snapshot of your company's overall status at a given point in time. SWOT is an acronym for **S**trengths, **W**eaknesses, **O**pportunities, and **T**hreats.

Tactic: an activity designed to achieve a desired result. Tactics are the things you do to implement a strategy. Where strategy describes "what," tactics describe "how to."

Threats: environmental trends with potentially negative impacts. Threats may impede implementation of strategy, increase risk, increase people or cash resources required, or cause us to reduce expectations for business results. Threats are also called risks.

Trade events: gatherings of business people designed to make marketing and selling cost-effective by bringing many buyers and sellers together under one roof. Examples include trade shows and conferences. Seminars, while focused on education, also are considered trade events.

Values statement: your code of ethics or the operating principles that are fundamental to your business and unlikely to change over a long period of time.

Vision statement: a short document that describes your view of the future of the industry or market. Vision statements are part predictions, part trend analysis, part context information.

Weaknesses: deficiencies that inhibit the ability to perform or achieve results, and must be overcome to avoid failure.

Working capital: the cash needed on hand to pay the expenses of your business, whether you are bringing in revenue from product sales or not.

For Further Study: Ten Classic (or Soon-to-Be Classic) Business Books

Want to learn more? A recent amazon.com search on the words "business planning" yielded over 5,000 (!) available book titles. Where to begin? The books listed below expand upon key business concepts discussed in *Succeeding in Music*. While they do not focus on the music industry, they include valuable lessons that can be helpful as you develop your music business.

Beckwith, Harry. *Selling the Invisible: A Field Guide to Modern Marketing.* New York: Warner Books, 1997.

Hawken, Paul. *Growing a Business: An Insider's Guide to Starting and Building a Business from the Ground Up.* New York: Fireside Books, 1998.

Kawasaki, Guy. *How to Drive Your Competition Crazy: Creating Disruption for Fun and Profit.* New York: Hyperion, 1996.

Moore, Geoffrey A. *Crossing the Chasm: Marketing and Selling Technology Products to Mainstream Customers.* New York: Harperbusiness, 1999.

Phillips, Michael, and Rasberry, Salli. *Marketing Without Advertising: Creative Strategies for Small Business Success.* Berkeley: Nolo Press, 2001.

Porter, Michael E. *Competitive Strategy: Techniques for Analyzing Industries and Competitors.* New York: Free Press, 1998.

Ries, Al, and Trout, Jack. *Positioning: The Battle for Your Mind.* New York: McGraw-Hill Professional Publishing, 2000.

Silber, Lee. *Time Management for the Creative Person: Right-Brain Strategies for Stopping Procrastination, Getting Control of the Clock & Calendar, and Freeing Up Your Time & Your Life.* New York: Three Rivers Press, 1998.

Tracy, Brian. *Maximum Achievement: Strategies and Skills That Will Unlock Your Hidden Powers to Succeed.* New York: Fireside Books, 1995.

Wolf, Michael J. *The Entertainment Economy: How Mega-Media Forces Are Transforming Our Lives.* New York: Times Books, 1999.

Music Industry Reference Books

Whether you are a performer, songwriter, agent, manager, or promoter, you can benefit from deeper knowledge of the music industry through studying music industry reference books. A recent amazon.com search on the words "music business" yielded over 400 (!) titles. As with the general business titles, it's easy to get bogged down because there are so many choices. Here are five recommended titles:

Avalon, Moses. *Confessions of a Record Producer: How to Survive the Scams and Shams of the Music Business.* San Francisco: Backbeat Books, 2002.

Brabec, Jeffrey, and Brabec, Todd. *Music, Money, and Success: The Insider's Guide to Making Money in the Music Industry.* New York: Schirmer Books, 2000.

Krasilovsky, M. William, et al. *This Business of Music: The Definitive Guide to the Music Industry.* New York: Watson-Guptill Publications, 2000.

Passman, Donald S. *All You Need to Know About the Music Business: Revised and Updated for the 21st Century.* New York: Simon & Schuster, 2000.

Weissman, Dick. *Making a Living In Your Local Music Market: Realizing Your Marketing Potential.* Milwaukee: Hal Leonard Corporation, 1999.

Web Resources

There are thousands of music-related magazines, websites, and trade organizations. To try to identify and evaluate all of them is futile at best.

Thankfully, with the ease of search engines on the Internet today, publishing a comprehensive directory in book form is unnecessary. For example, a simple Internet search on the keywords "bluegrass+music+business" yielded over 80,000 (!) listings.

Still, there are some magazines and trade groups that cross genre boundaries and are useful to anyone in the music business. Here are ten web resources that are relevant to performers, songwriters, agents, managers, and promoters:

General Information

1. List of music journals, newspapers, and periodicals: www.music.indiana.edu/music_resources/journals.html
2. Pollstar—The Music Hotwire: www.pollstar.com
3. *Billboard* magazine: www.billboard.com

Performing Rights Organizations (PROs)

4. American Society of Composers, Authors, and Publishers (ASCAP): www.ascap.com
5. BMI: www.bmi.com
6. SESAC: www.sesac.com
7. Society of Composers, Authors, and Music Publishers of Canada (SOCAN): www.socan.ca

Unions and Trade Organizations

8. American Federation of Musicians of the United States and Canada (AFM): www.afm.org
9. National Academy of Recording Arts and Sciences (NARAS): www.grammy.com
10. National Music Publishers Association (NMPA): www.nmpa.org

CD-ROM Contents

The CD-ROM that accompanies this book is a great tool for getting started on your business plan. The disc includes the following:

Section 1: Industry Reference Material

- Glossary of key terms, concepts, and buzzwords
- List of general business and music business books
- Web links for music trade magazines and trade associations

Section 2: Business Plan Templates

- Vision, mission, and values statement
- Risk analysis checklist
- Short-form business plan outline
- Brand positioning statement
- Three-year product plan and sales forecast matrix
- Sources and uses of working capital
- Goal-setting and milestone-tracking sheet
- "Our Band" business plan

Section 3: Link to www.succeedinginmusic.net

This website is the online focal point of a community or network of music people (performers, songwriters, agents, managers, promoters).

As someone who has purchased and read *Succeeding in Music*, you are qualified for a free membership in the network. Follow the link on the CD-ROM, or go to www.succeedinginmusic.net via your web browser.

The site includes the following features:

- White papers for download or online viewing
- Information on new books, videos, and live seminars
- Online forum for "members" to post questions and conduct listserv-style discussions
- Online reference material including glossary of business terms and music business bibliography
- Links to music industry sites, publisher partners, and trade organizations

Join today!

INDEX

A

accountants, 6
accounting, finance, 34
action list
    business plan and, 56
advertising, 84, 183
    as promotional tool, 84–85
    sample promotion plan and, 162
    types of, 84–85
    by word of mouth, 87
AFM. *See* American Federation of Musicians
agent(s), 5, 7
    advertising and, 85
    buying habits, preferences of, 109
    collateral materials and, 86
    competition and, 116
    creative goals and, 126–127
    creative goals worksheet for, 174
    distribution channels for, 95
    financial goals worksheet for, 175
    as influencers, 88
    job description of, 21
    market for, 21
    payment for, 22
    personal goals worksheet for, 176–177
    sales literature and, 86
    salesforce strategy and, 99
    showcase performances and, 90
amateur, 183
    professional vs., 12
American Federation of Musicians (AFM), 25, 61
Armstrong, Louis, 73
art, 183
    commerce vs., 14
artistic integrity
    commercial viability and, 151
ASCAP, 22, 25, 61
assumption, 183
"attention management," 62
audience, 183

B

balance sheet, 183
"Behind the Music," 6
Bennett, Tony, 73
Billboard charts, 11
Billboard magazine, 84

BMG Entertainment, 27
BMI, 22, 25, 61
booking agent(s), 6
    music business products of, 70
    pricing strategy of, 76
brand building, 143
brand positioning statement
    business plan and, 51, 52–54, 55
    "elevator test" and, 54
    example of, 157–158
    purpose of, 52
    uses for, 53–54
    worksheet for, 167
branding, 83–84, 183
Brooks, Garth, 6
budget, 183
business
    management of, 154
business lessons
    importance of sales and, 139
    for music world, 137–142
    quantifying of, 137–138
    strengths, weaknesses and, 139–140
    understanding competition and, 141–142
    understanding of customers and, 140–141
    weaknesses and, 138–139
business plan, 35, 183
    action list and, 56
    appendix for, 49
    application of fundamentals for, 143–144
    assumptions of, 46–47
    benefits of, 39–42
    brand building and, 143
    brand positioning statement and, 52–54, 157-158
    cash and, 145
    as catalyst, 41
    company description and, 46
    as competitive weapon, 42
    contents checklist for, 166
    creation of, 143
    elements of, 45, 143–144
    financial summary and, 46, 164
    five "chapters" of, 45–46
    frequently asked questions and, 145–147
    function of, 39
    as fund-raising tool, 42
    importance of, 39–42
    length, detail of, 48–49

making decisions and, 143
management team and, 46
market overview and, 46, 158
marketing strategy and, 46, 48, 160-163
as measuring stick, 40
"memory system" and, 45
mission statement and, 51–52
operating plan and, 55
operations, infrastructure for, 159–160
as opportunity management tool, 40–41
organization overview and, 46
percentage breakdown of, 47–48
planning flow and, 51, 57
product description and, 46
product plan and, 54–55, 158–159
as road map, 40
sample of, 156–163
as stress management tool, 41
as team-building tool, 42
team organization for, 159
business services
product strategy and, 69, 70
buyer characteristics, 183
buying public, 28

C

career, 183
hobby vs., 12
catalog, 61
"channel of distribution"
marketing strategy and, 94–95
cold canvassing, 87. *See also* missionary selling
collateral. *See* collateral material(s)
collateral material(s), 183
as promotional tool, 86
sample promotion plan and, 162
commerce, 183
art vs., 14
commercial viability
artistic integrity and, 151
common sense lessons,
of music industry, 149–153
competition, 154
competitive intelligence and, 119–120
customer profiles and, 116
"external environment" and, 118–119
"internal environment" and, 118–119
standing out from, 151–152
SWOT analysis and, 118–119
understanding of, 115–122, 141–142
competitive intelligence system, 183
sources of information for, 119–120
competitive profiles, 120
composer(s), 7, 21. *See also* songwriter(s)
concert, event promoters, 7
corporate music business, 26
corporation, 183
creative goals, 126–127, 183
agents, managers worksheet for, 174
performer, songwriter worksheet for, 170

creative objectives, 129–130
customer profile(s)
buying habits, preferences and, 109
competition and, 116
economic information and, 107–108
geographic information and, 108
individual vs. institutional customers and,
109–110
market segmentation and, 110–111
psychographic information and, 108
target customers and, 111–112
understanding of, 107–108
customer segments, 111
customer(s), 183-184
style and, 108–109
understanding of, 140–141

D

daily action list
business plan and, 51
day job, 183
deal-breakers
non-viable customers and, 110, 112
deep catalog, 61
demo recordings
as promotional tool, 86
demographic information, 184
customer profile and, 107
differentiation, 184
direct competition, 184
identification of, 116
indirect competition vs., 28, 115–116, 118
sample marketing plan and, 163
direct mail, 86
direct marketing, 86–87, 184
sample promotion plan and, 162
telemarketing and, 87

E

e-business. *See* e-commerce
e-commerce, 184
as promotional tool, 90
sample promotion plan and, 163
economic information, 184
"elevator test," 184
brand positioning statement and, 54
Ellington, Duke, 73
EMI Music, 27
end-user segments
sample marketing plan and, 163
entertainment, 184
self-expression vs., 14
event producer
market for, 21–22
event promoters, 6, 8
executive summary, 184

F

financial goals, 126–127, 127–128, 184
agents, managers worksheet for, 175

performer, songwriter worksheet for, 170
financial objectives, 130, 131–132. *See also* sales revenue
Fitzgerald, Ella, 73
full-time, 184
    part-time *vs.*, 12
fundamentals of business
    music and, 1–2

G

Gavin, 85
geographic information, 184
geographical territory
    sample marketing plan and, 163
goal(s), 184
    categories of, 126
    creative goals and, 126–127, 170, 174, 183
    financial goals and, 126, 127–128, 170, 175, 184
    importance of, 125
    in music business, 154
    objectives vs., 13, 125–126
    personal goals and, 128, 170, 173, 176-177, 185
    quantifying objectives and, 129–130
    sharing of, 134
Guitar Player, 85

H

hobby, 184
    career vs., 12
hybrid, 184

I

identity item(s), 184
    as promotional tools, 89
    sample promotion plan and, 163
income statement, 184
independent "indie" label, 184
independent music business, 26
indirect competition, 184
    direct competition vs., 28, 115–116, 118
    threat to, 28–29
    understanding of, 116–117
individual customers, 184
influencers, 185
infrastructure
    example of, 159–160
institutional customers, 185
integrity
    sales and, 100–101
International Bluegrass Music Association (IBMA), 1

J

James, Etta, 73

K

key influencer relations, 88–89
    sample promotion plan and, 163
King, B.B., 6, 73

L

Limited Liability Company (LLC), 185
    in music industry, 26
Limited Liability Partnership (LLP), 185
    in music industry, 26
links in marketing chain, 185
live performances
    product strategy and, 69, 70
low-cost producer, 185

M

Madonna, 76
major label, 185
management, 185
    key responsibilities of, 35
manager(s), 5, 7, 8
    advertising and, 85
    buying habits, preferences of, 109
    collateral materials and, 86
    competition and, 116
    creative goals and, 126–127
    creative goals worksheet for, 174
    distribution channels for, 95
    financial goals worksheet for, 175
    as influencers, 88
    job description of, 21
    market for, 21
    music business products of, 70
    personal goals worksheet for, 176–177
    pricing strategy of, 76
    sales literature and, 86
    salesforce strategy and, 99
    showcase performances and, 90
market
    assessment of, 21–22
market overview, 158
market segmentation, 185
marketing, 34, 63, 185
    advertising, promotion and, 64
    communication with target market and, 64
    competition and, 115–122
    customer relationships and, 64
    functions of, 63–64
    pricing strategy and, 66, 75–82
    product planning, positioning and, 63
    product strategy and, 66
    promotional strategy and, 66, 83–92
marketing challenge
    competition and, 151–152
marketing functions, 185
marketing plan
    competitive profiles and, 120
    example of, 160–163
marketing strategy
    channel, venue type and, 94–95
    customer profile and, 107–108
    customers and, 107–113
    geographical area for, 93–94
    individual vs. institutional customers and, 109–110
    market segmentation and, 110–111
    nonviable customers and, 110

"place" and, 93–97
salesforce strategy and, 99–105
style and, 108–109
workspace and, 95–97
Marley, Bob, 6
McEuen, John, ix
mid-line releases, 73
mission
    in music business, 154
    sample business plan and, 156
mission statement, 185
    business plan and, 51–52, 55
    excerpts from, 15
    purpose of, 15–16
    writing of, 16–17
missionary selling
    as promotional tool, 84
Monroe, Bill, 73
MP3.com, 25, 61
music industry, 11
    accounting, finance and, 34
    amateur vs. professional in, 12–13
    art vs. commerce and, 14
    aspirations, motivations in, 11–12
    business lessons for, 137–142
    business problems of, 5–6
    careers in, 7–8
    common sense lessons of, 149–153
    competitive environment of, 28–29, 62
    corporate vs. independent businesses within, 27
    customers of, 27–28
    entertainment vs. self-expression in, 14
    full-time vs. part-time in, 12
    fundamentals of business and, 1
    goals vs. objectives in, 13
    goods and services in, 69–70
    hobby vs. career within, 12
    industry role, product and, 55, 69
    key elements of, 21–23, 34–35
    management and, 35
    media and, 6, 7
    myths, realities of, 27
    overview of, 25–26
    product delivery and, 34
    product development and, 34
    product pricing within, 80–81
    record labels and, 7
    revenue stream in, 22
    risk and, 20, 21, 31–36
    sales, marketing and, 34, 62-63
    starting in, 19–23
    statistics of, 61–62
    strategic questions in, 19–20
    strategies vs. tactics in, 13
    target market for, 21–22
    working capital for, 32–34
music publisher(s), 7
    buying habits, preferences of, 109
music publishing
    product strategy and, 69, 70
music teachers, 7

N
New Yorker, The, 85
nonviable customers
    marketing strategy and, 110
Northern America
    music business in, 25

O
objective(s), 185
    creation of goals and, 129–130
    goals vs., 13, 125–126
    in music business, 154
operating plan
    business plan and, 51, 55
    checklist for, 168
    creation of, 169
    elements of, 56
    revisions to, 57
opportunities, 185

P
partnership, 185
    in music industry, 26
part-time, 185
    full-time vs., 12
Paul, Les, 73
Pavarotti, Luciano, 6
performer(s), 5
    collateral materials and, 86
    creative goals worksheet for, 170
    description of, 21
    distribution channels for, 94
    financial goals worksheet for, 170
    as influencers, 88
    market for, 21
    payment for, 22
    personal goals worksheet for, 170–173
    sales literature and, 86
    salesforce strategy and, 99
    showcase performances and, 90
personal goals, 128, 185
    agent, manager worksheet for, 176–177
    performer, songwriter worksheet for, 170–173
personal managers, 6
personal objectives, 130
"place," 93-97
place strategy, 185
    evolution of, 97
planning
    as business investment, 149–150
    implementation and, 154
planning flow, 185
    business plan and, 51, 57
pricing strategy
    avoidance of problems with, 81
    conventions, traditions of, 76–77
    differentiation and, 78
    example of, 162
    factors of, 75–77
    hybrid strategy and, 78–79

low-cost producer strategy and, 77–78
    revenue planning and, 79–80
    sales, marketing ability and, 77
    supply, demand and, 76
private corporations, 26-27
product, 186
product delivery, 34
product development, 34, 186
product life cycle, 186
    phases of, 72–74
product mix
    example of, 162
product plan
    business plan and, 51, 54–55
    example of, 158–159
    revisions to, 57
    worksheet for, 168
product strategy
    business plan and, 55
    business services and, 69, 70
    development of, 69–74
    live performances and, 69, 70
    music publishing and, 69, 70
    product "life cycle" and, 72–74
    record sales and, 69, 70
    technical services and, 69, 70
    worksheet for, 71
professional, 186
    amateur vs., 12
profit, 14, 186
    music people and, 14–15
promoter(s), 5
    advertising and, 85
    buying habits, preferences of, 109
    collateral materials and, 86
    competition and, 116
    creative goals and, 126–127
    creative goals worksheet for, 178
    distribution channels for, 95
    financial goals worksheet for, 179
    as influencers, 88
    job description of, 21
    market for, 21–22
    music business products of, 70
    payment for, 22
    personal goals worksheet for, 180–182
    sales literature and, 86
    salesforce strategy and, 100
    showcase performances and, 90
promotion, 83
promotion plan
    example of, 162–163
promotional strategy
    advertising and, 83, 84–85
    branding and, 83–84
    key questions for, 91
    promotion and, 83
promotional toolbox, 186
promotional tools
    collateral and, 86

demo recording and, 86
direct marketing as, 86–87
e-commerce as, 90
identity items and, 89
key influencer relations and, 88–89
missionary selling as, 84
publicity as, 85
sales literature and, 85
showcase performances and, 89
trade events and, 87–88
types of, 84–91
"word of mouth" and, 84
psychographic information, 186
public corporations, 26, 186
publicists, 7
publicity, 186
    purpose of, 85
    sample promotion plan and, 162
publicly traded company. *See* public corporation

R
Radio and Records, 85
record industry
    pricing conventions in, 76
record label executive(s)
    as influencers, 88
record labels, 7, 184-185
record producer(s), 6
    buying habits, preferences of, 109
record sales
    product strategy and, 69, 70
revenue, 186
    definition of, 79
    optimization of, 81
revenue planning, 79–80
revenue stream, 186
reward
    risk vs., 20
risk, 186
    tolerance for, 152–153, 154
risk analysis, 31–36, 186
    assessment of, 19–20
    checklist for, 165
    perspective on, 31
    reward *vs.*, 20–21
risk spectrum, 31–32
Rolling Stone Magazine, 6, 85
Rolling Stones, 76
royalties, 22

S
sales, 34, 186
    achievement of objectives for, 64–65
    administrative tasks of, 65
    competitive environment and, 66
    definition of, 63
    end-user profiles and, 66
    event participation and, 65
    functions of, 64–65
    sales channel strategy and, 66

sales force strategy and, 66
territory management and, 65
sales functions, 186
sales literature, 186
as promotional tool, 86
sample promotion plan and, 162
sales revenue
forecasting of, 132–133
salesforce
capacity and, 101, 102–103
chemistry and, 103
competence and, 101, 102
music product and, 103–104
"three c's" and, 101–103
salesforce strategy
integrity and, 100–101
marketing and, 99–105
marketing plan sample and, 163
salesperson characteristics and, 101
schoolteacher paradigm, 131–132
Seeger, Pete, 73
self-expression, 186
entertainment vs., 14
selling strategy
example of, 162
SESAC, 22, 25, 61
shake-out, 72
showcase performance(s), 186
as promotional tools, 89
promotion plan sample and, 163
sole proprietorship, 186
in music industry, 26
songwriter(s), 5, 6, 7, 21
advertising and, 85
competition and, 116
creative goals worksheet for, 170
distribution channels for, 95
financial goals worksheet for, 170
market for, 21
music business products of, 70
payment for, 22
personal goals worksheet for, 170–173
pricing strategy of, 76
sales literature and, 86
salesforce strategy and, 99
showcase performances and, 90
Sony Music Entertainment, 27
SoundScan, 61
Spears, Britney, 6
Stern, Issac, 73
strategy, 186
tactics vs., 13, 126
Streisand, Barbra, 76
strengths, 186
studio musicians, 8
supply and demand, 187
SWOT analysis, 187
competition and, 118–119

T
tactic(s), 187
strategy vs., 13, 126
target customer, 21. *See also* market
team organization
example of, 159
technical services
product strategy and, 69, 70
technicians
pricing strategy of, 76
telemarketing
direct marketing and, 87
threats, 187
"trackability," 87
trade events, 187
conferences and, 87
opportunities at, 88
as promotional tool, 87–88
seminars and, 87–88
trade shows and, 87
trade shows
sample promotion plan and, 163

U
U2, 6
Universal Music Group, 27
USA Today, 6
Utne Reader, 85

V
values
sample business plan and, 156
values statement, 187
excerpt from, 16
purpose of, 15
VH1, 6
vision
for career, 154
sample business plan and, 156
vision statement, 187
excerpts from, 16
purpose of, 15

W
Warner Music Group, 27
weaknesses, 187
Wired, 85
word of mouth, 84
as advertising, 85, 87
working capital, 187
sources of, 33–34
working musicians, 7
workspace
marketing strategy and, 95–97

Y
Yankovic, Frankie, 73

ABOUT THE AUTHOR

John Stiernberg is founder and principal consultant of Stiernberg Consulting, a Sherman Oaks, California–based business development firm. John has more than twenty-five years of experience in the music and entertainment technology fields. He currently works with a variety of business clients on strategic planning and market development projects.

Prior to establishing Stiernberg Consulting in 1993, John worked for audio-equipment manufacturers for twelve years in sales, marketing, and general management. He has managed salesforces, launched products, developed staff organizations, and written business plans for those companies and more than fifty private clients.

From 1973 to 1981, John was a professional musician, booking agent, and part owner of a music retail store. As a performer on acoustic guitar and five-string banjo, he has appeared on stage, records, television, and radio.

John received a B.A. (magna cum laude/Phi Beta Kappa) in music and anthropology from Ripon College in 1973. He is a member of NAMM, NSCA, and CEDIA, as well as a voting member of NARAS, the American Federation of Musicians, the North American Folk Music and Dance Alliance, and the International Bluegrass Music Association.

In addition to strategic planning and industry analysis, John is in demand as a keynote speaker and seminar presenter. He was named NSCA Educator of the Year in May 2000. He presents seminars and writes articles, and he is planning a series of educational video programs based on *Succeeding in Music* called "Business Chops for Music People."

For more information, including a complete list of publications and original seminars, please visit www.succeedinginmusic.net, or e-mail John at askjohn@succeedinginmusic.net.

Serious Players.

The Music Player Network is for serious players. From guitars, bass, keyboards and recording to computer music culture, dance, trance and more. • Our industry-leading magazines, *Guitar Player*, *Keyboard*, *Bass Player*, *Gig*, *MC²*, *Rumble*, *EQ* and *Extreme Groove*, take the art of playing music seriously. And so does our leading portal website, MusicPlayer.com. • Our editors and writers are experienced musicians and engineers with special insights and hands-on experience that only comes from real-time playing. • If you want to get serious about your playing, check us out at your nearest newsstand or visit MusicPlayer.com on the web.